Fortified City

Robin Roundtree

DOD Publications

Fortified City by Robin Roundtree
Published by DOD Publications LLC.

Unless otherwise indicated, all scripture quotations are taken from the King James Version (KJV) of the Holy Bible.

The events and people described in this book are based on actual experiences of or shared with the author. However, the names of some people and places have been either changed or omitted.

ISBN: 978-1-967603-01-5 (paperback)

Printed in the United States of America

DEDICATION

To the Almighty and Everlasting God our Father

To Jesus, our Savior, Lord, Light, and Salvation

To the Holy Spirit, the Divine breath of God, for the words of this book

To my Parents, Reuben and Eddis Roundtree Sr., who have taught me lessons of enduring love with their 74 years of marriage

To my beloved siblings, Ruby, Reuben Jr (wife Shirley), Jimmie, Regina, Reginald and Jerissa

To my wonderful children, Keiara Venise, Jerome Courtney Jr (wife Tae), Lorenda Irene, Anthony Denzel, Angel Marie, and Amera Beatrice

To my beautiful grandchildren, Malachi, Josiah, Israel, Chozen, Sunshyne, Jerome III, Keeng, Ace, Ty, De'lariece, Robert Jr, Rylee, Raymone, Royce, Roddrick, Nevaeh, Kelly III, Karmine, Kayden, and Amer

To my handsome great-grandson Louis

To my Apostles for preaching the Word of God without compromising and the awesome Breakthrough Ministries Int'l church family in Wichita, Kansas

To Angela Gegen, Odessa Scruggs, Janice Parks, Veneda Brown, Elizabeth McMeans, Renee Davis, for your special "sistah" girl love

To Chukwuma Christopher Nwankwo, for your wisdom, encouragement, and support from afar

To Dr. Peggy Pugh and Shelly Garrison, who prophesied, WRITE THE BOOK.

Contents

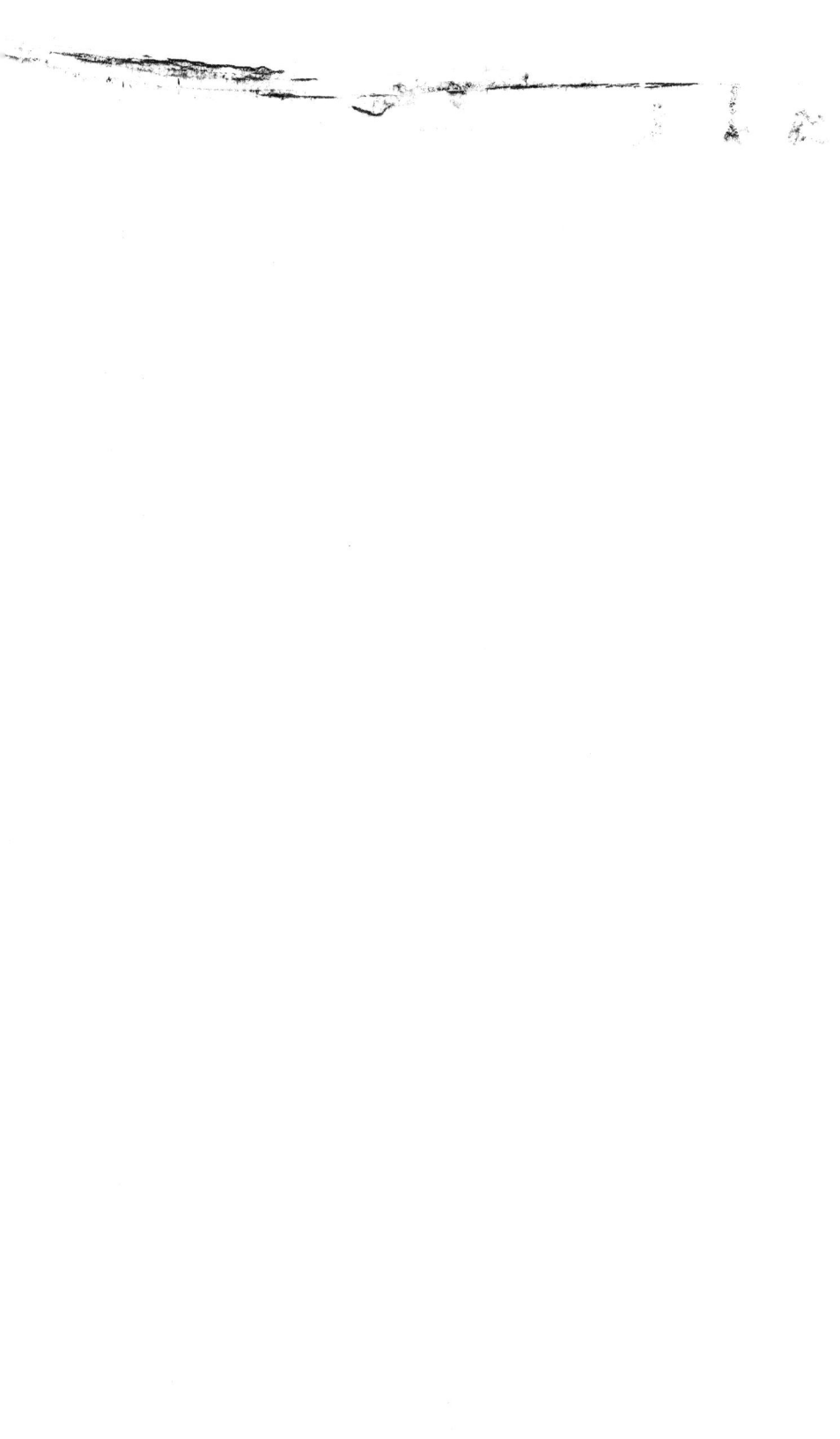

INTRODUCTION

Sometimes it is about you. But not in the way you, at times, desire. This book is way past due and right on time. I admit I had to repent in the latter part of 2024 when God gave me an ultimatum. He asked me, "Do you want someone else to write the book I told you to write?" My answer, of course, was "no" as I pictured myself opening a book similar to this one with another Author's name. It's definitely not something I want to experience. Honestly, I found myself ashamed as I began to start again for the "umteenth" time. Why had I put God's work aside like it had no importance, forgetting that although it wasn't about me, it was! It's about me because I have lives to touch and no one can touch the people that I am supposed to reach like I can because God equipped me in a unique way to do so.

Fortified City is an extension of the sermon I preached during Nightwatch (New Year's Eve) Service, December 31, 2007, entitled, "The Eighth Day". I was told to write this book shortly after this date, which gives you an idea of how long God has been merciful to me. If I haven't learned nothing else from this experience, I've learned just how important I am as a city of light!

14) Ye are the light of the world. A city that is set on an hill cannot be hid.

15) Neither do men light a candle, and put it under a bushel, but on a candlestick; and it giveth light unto all that are in the house. 16) Let your light so shine before men, that they may see your good works, and glorify your Father which is in heaven. (Matthew 5:14-16).

Chapter 1

CITY LIGHTS

Understand that your presence in this world is no small thing. It matters! It is often said that if we all could reach out and help just one person, the world would be a better place. But truthfully, unless the recipient dies after their encounter with us, we never reach just one. We touch generations and generations to come. The domino effect happens when we share the light of Jesus with others, and in turn, they share, and so on and so on.

"Ye are the light of the world...". What does it mean to be a light, and where does the light come from? John 8:12 says, *"Then spake Jesus again unto them, saying, I am the light of the world: he that followeth me shall not walk in darkness, but shall have the light of life."* The light within comes from following Jesus! Jesus made it clear in this verse that not only is He the light, but He is also the life!

Life, according to the biblical definition, is the Greek word zão, which means *"to live, breathe, be among the living (not lifeless, not dead) and to enjoy real life"* (Thayer's Greek Lexicon). We are not here just to exist. We are to be active beings, full of vigor and operating through the power of the Holy Spirit. If we stay in tune with the Holy Spirit, we can always be sure of our steps.

The light of Jesus in us can't be hidden. It's always evident. It can't help itself. Once you accept Jesus into your life, it's like walking around with a built-in lantern full of oil! Darkness moves out of the way when the light comes on the scene, revealing everything the darkness tried to hide.

Let's revisit John 8:12. *"Then spake Jesus again unto them, saying, I am the light of the world: he that followeth me shall not walk in darkness, but shall have the light of life."* So, how can we be the light of the world if Jesus is the light of the world? Imagine standing on a stage and the spotlight is right on you. Chances are, you can't see the person who is shining it on you, just the light, and everyone in the audience can't see the people in the dark, but they can see you perfectly. That's how it is when we follow Jesus. We stand in the ray of His light and become lit up with a silent boast of Jesus' presence!

It is the presence of Jesus' light within us that makes us a city. As a Believer (a follower of Jesus), we spread the love of God through His Son by doing what God created us to do, which doesn't call for a lot of "Pomp and Circumstance", just obedience.

The purpose of this book is to take a deeper look at your significance in this world by seeing yourself as a brightly lit city. In the pages ahead, you will learn the names of several fortified cities in the Bible and their meanings. You will be able to identify which one you represent by their description. You may find that you have the characteristics of more than one, or that your city changes from one season of your life to another.

This book was written with both the Believer and the Unbeliever in mind. A Believer may know many, or all the stories shared within the pages, but remember that the Unbeliever may not, so if you're a Believer, enjoy them as a refresher.

There are some cities chosen for the book that are not fortified and are noted beneath the title. I felt led to include them because metaphorically, they represent a type of fortification. For example, all six Cities of Refuge are included because a place of refuge provides safety and strength. Finally, for cities that have no formal name for their citizens past or present, I have added "ite or ene" to the ending of their name to help the reader personalize it for themselves. All verses are from the King James Version unless otherwise noted.

What is a fortified City?

Chapter 2

GOD'S PROMISE TO JEREMIAH

For, behold, I have made thee this day a defenced city, and an iron pillar, and brasen walls against the whole land, against the kings of Judah, against the princes thereof, against the priests thereof, and against the people of the land. Jeremiah 1:18 KJV

For behold, I have made you this day A fortified city and an iron pillar, And bronze walls against the whole land--Against the kings of Judah, Against its princes, Against its priests, And against the people of the land. Jeremiah 1:18 NKJV

FOR BEHOLD

"Behold!" says the fake TV artist as he yanks the perfectly draped satin sheet from the beautifully colorful painted portrait resting upon a cast iron easel. It's the word that is said before the unveiling of something great or spectacular.

If you're a parent, more than likely, you can agree that the first time you laid eyes on your newborn baby, there was nothing more beautiful and precious in the whole wide world. That sweet, untainted newborn smell and soft, silky skin were irresistible to touch and kiss.

It used to be that a woman would have to wait for six weeks before leaving the house after the birth of a baby, giving enough time for her body to recover and heal. Let me be the first to tell you that my mother, Eddis Roundtree, didn't play about that! It was six weeks, with no exceptions, and the baby better not be around people breathing all over it either. She was a registered nurse, so that was what was expected. As a new mother, once you had the opportunity to show off your new bundle of joy, you couldn't wait.

Depending upon the weather, you presumably covered him or her with a blanket or hooded carrier to hide them from the sun and rain, or cold. You learned quickly that you were no longer the most important person in the room. It was your newborn. Whether you came to their house or they came to yours, you became invisible to your friends or loved ones. The first thing they would blurt out upon seeing you was "Where's the baby?" And just like an artist revealing his treasured painting, you pulled the covering off the baby, allowing adoration of this sweet, precious being. Your child was and is the apple of your eye, just as we are the apple of God's eye. He presents us to others with a salutation of "Behold", and with that word, he rested a light upon your countenance so that you would one day understand your importance in this world. Shine your light!

I HAVE MADE THEE

The Bible is the most intriguing book that has ever existed. Within its pages, the God of all gods, the Creator of the universe, shows His sovereignty from Genesis to Revelation.

The Bible is the only book that not only holds all truth but is an actual "living word". Let me explain what I mean when I say a living word. Imagine, for a moment, spilling one cup of water on your kitchen table. It didn't look like much when you poured it into your drinking glass, but before you can get a paper towel to clean up the mess it made, you discover that it has spread from where the glass was sitting, clear to the end of the table, and is now dripping on the floor. The table is wet, the tipped-over cup is wet, the chair seat and floor are too, and you have one paper towel trying to absorb it all in one wipe. That's how the power of the Word of God (Bible aka Living Word) works! It affects you and everything around you. With all our earthly knowledge, it cannot be absorbed or contained in just one study. It revitalizes your total being, from the inside out. It's not just a book; it's a transformer that nourishes and guides its reader.

The Bible story of Moses and Pharaoh is one that proves God's eminence. In the Book of Exodus, Israelites had been enslaved under the relentless rulership of Pharaoh for 400 years. Moses came as an arm of God to implore him to release the Israelites. Each time Pharaoh refused, Egypt would be overtaken by a plague, ten altogether. But amid this event, God hardened Pharaoh's heart and caused him to rebel. Some have questioned God's reason for doing such a thing, but in my opinion, part of the reason was to show his ascendancy! Pharaoh was so harsh towards the Israelite slaves, yet he could not control his own heart!

Genesis 2:7 says, *"And God formed man of the dust of the ground and breathed into his nostrils the breath of life; and man became a living soul."* God made us! He made every organ, every bone, every muscle, every cell, our characteristics, our giftings, everything! So why wouldn't the one who created us, be able to control our heart, if He so desires? Isn't He the one who causes blood to flow through it and beat? There is, of course, only one answer: yes!

Pharaoh, in all his arrogance, couldn't control his own heart and soon learned, by losing his firstborn son (the tenth and final plague), that he could not bring his son to breathe again. Even today, some people think that with enough money and fame, they can do anything they please. They've become their own god, yet they cannot control their ability to breathe in and out and out and in continuously every second of their lives. Only God of all creation; *"...the world, and they that dwell therein"* (Exodus 24:1), the One who knew us *"Before I formed thee in the belly..."* (Jeremiah 1:5), and gave us a future, or *"...an expected end"* (Jeremiah 29:11), can do that because He made us!

THIS DAY

I don't care how old you are, the generation before you has boasted about how things "used to be" as if it didn't come with hard times for its day. Most of us have a day or season we would love to step back into and relive. But we all need to understand that we're made and equipped for the time in which we live.

It's okay to talk about the "good ole' days" to youngsters but do it without the desire to punish them for not going through what you went through. Sure, the schools didn't close every time it snowed more than five inches. Of course, you didn't stay home each time you got the sniffles. Yes, you had to pick cotton and plow the field before having breakfast. Just be proud that it made you the strong person you are today. Believe me when I say, these kids nowadays have far worse worries, despite all their modern conveniences.

Some of our grandparents were born to withstand the days of the Great Depression, and some lived through the generation of the civil rights movement. The present generations are empowered to keep fighting for injustices while enjoying the inventions and equality you may have helped to bring about. At the end of the day, whatever your season of life, know that as long as we are alive, we stand on the battlefield of God, till we die!

The Fortified City

A DEFENCED CITY

(A Fortified City)

A defenced city, according to StudyLights.org, Holman Bible Dictionary, "refers to a town with strong defenses, usually a massive wall structure and inner citadels (a fortress on higher ground), or strongholds. In general, the fortified city was a major military or administrative center for a region."

The Great Wall of China is a wall that was built to protect China from tribal nomadic invaders of ancient times, known as Genghis Khan. "Genghis Khan, also known as Chinggis Khan, was the founder and first Khan of the Mongol Empire" (Wikipedia.org). A Khan was simply a Mongol Ruler. Emperor Qin Shi Huangdi was the one who decided to build this wall which took from 7 B.C. to 17 A.D. to construct and is a span of 13,171 miles long.

The United States is only about 2,800 miles wide east to west, making the Great Wall of China five times its width. You would come closer in size if you compared the Wall to the measurement of North America's entire perimeter, which is approximately 12,000 miles.

Picture the U.S. continent and imagine for a moment being encircled by a wall that connects completely around its borders. Now go smaller and picture it around your state, city, neighborhood, home, family, loved ones, and finally, you. What about around your mind, heart, or ears? God fortifies (protects, secures, and strengthens) you just as a wall around the borders of a city, that keeps its citizens safe from its enemy. His protection exceeds these things.

Zechariah 2:5 says, "For I, saith the Lord, will be unto her a wall of fire round about, and will be the glory in the midst of her (Jerusalem)." Also, Psalm 125:2 says, *As the mountains are round about Jerusalem, so the Lord is round about his people from henceforth even for ever."* We can walk in confidence and exercise in God's will when we understand we are a strong (fortified) city because we possess a defense that is like nothing on earth because it is *the LORD strong and mighty"* (Psalm 24:8b) all by Himself!

AN IRON PILLAR

There is an iron pillar that stands in the Qutb complex at Mehrauli in Delhi, India. Resembling the cast iron yard light, popular in the 70s, it is nothing special to look at, but it has a very interesting history. Said to have been built by King Chandragupta II around 400 C.E., it is famous for its rust-resistant composition. It stands 20 feet tall with an additional 3 feet and 8 inches below ground and weighs approximately 6 tons.

There is a chemistry term called "waters of crystallization," where water molecules are present inside crystals, usually present but not bonded to a metal coordinate compound. They provide for the invisible protective layer known as miswrite. This compound of hydrogen, iron, and oxygen makes the pillar resistant to corrosion.

Now enough of the scientific stuff, which is, to most of us, way over our heads! My real point is to show the type of strength Jeremiah was said to possess. Bible readers know that Jeremiah was called the "weeping prophet" because of the burden he carried for his people, the Israelites. When God said to him, *"I will make you a defenced city, and an iron pillar",* He wasn't talking about a physical city or a physical iron pillar, like the one in Delhi, India. He was talking about Jeremiah.

In 1982, my parents, Reuben and Eddis Roundtree, moved to Bel Aire, Kansas, which is a suburban city right outside of the northeast end of Wichita. We had a few racially motivated incidents. One was a situation with neighbors who had sons who owned race cars. On two separate occasions, they purposely ran over our mailbox with one of the cars. After the second time, my dad put the mailbox on an iron post that stabilized about six feet underground. If they had chosen to try and run the mailbox over again, their race car would have shown the hard evidence! Right today, forty-three years later, that same post holds their mailbox.

What God was trying to let Jeremiah know was that He would cause him to be as tough as iron and strong as a pillar. Even though Jeremiah didn't feel capable of following through with the charge he was given by God, he would be made to withstand even his toughest enemy and greatest trials. God would be right there with him to help him endure the rejection that was sure to come.

As God's messengers, whether in action or by words, we can rest assured that God is on our side. All we have to do is be *"stedfast, unmoveable, always abounding in the work of the Lord, forasmuch as ye know that your labour is not in vain in the Lord." (1 Cor 15:58)*

BRAZEN WALLS

Brazen is a word that simply means something made of brass. Brass is a compound of mostly copper and zinc, not to be confused with bronze, which is made up of copper with tin. Zinc gives brass its yellow tone, just as tin gives bronze its reddish tone. Zinc makes copper stronger, and tin gives bronze more strength.

I am clarifying between these words because the King James version uses the words brazen walls and the New King James version uses the word bronze, but both are strong and durable metals. What God was letting Jeremiah know in a nutshell was that he would give him a ministry of great strength and endurance.

There is a scripture found in Micah 4:13 that says, *"Arise and thresh, O daughter of Zion: for I will make thine horn iron, and I will make thy hoofs brass: and thou shalt beat in pieces many people:"*. It came to mind as I was writing this section, only because it was the subject verse of the very first sermon I preached entitled, "Wrecked, Reconstructed and Revived, Equipped for God's Agenda" back in 2002. I won't go into details about that sermon (that's another book for another time). But the main point and purpose of the sermon was to share that God will give us strength and endurance (horns of iron and hooves of bronze) to do whatever he has assigned us to do. We don't have to worry about the giants when we grow to understand our confidence rests in the One who has us walled in from every direction!

AGAINST THE WHOLE LAND

"What shall we then say to the things? If God be for us, who shall be against us?" (Romans 8:31) Jeremiah had to gird himself and stand flat-footed to speak words of warning to the very people he passionately loved at the risk of losing his own life. The land of Judah was described in a way that could be compared to our modern days. The people of the land were just as unruly, disrespectful, and ungodly as the people of current times. No regard for God or the people of God exists. But God, in all His power and glory, bestowed upon us the ability to withstand every evil attempt upon our life and causes us to stand resilient! Whether we are dealing with Kings, future Kings (princes), Priests, Pastors, or the common man, we can be assured that with God on our side, we will undoubtedly be victorious! Though the enemy will do his best to wear us down, from one generation to the next, we (the people of God) will finish strong!

"And they shall fight against thee; but they shall not prevail against thee; for I am with thee, saith the Lord, to deliver thee. (Jeremiah 1:19)

What City Are You?

Chapter 3

CITY OF BETHLEHEM

House of Bread, House of War, Both to War and to Eat

Fortified by King Rehoboam

But when Peter was come to Antioch, I withstood him to the face, because he was to be blamed. (Galatians 2:11 KJV)

I heard politicians say that although they may have a friend who is on the opposite side of their political party, they can still sit down and have lunch together. Coming from a family of many denominations, I can relate to that thought process. Growing up Baptist and becoming Pentecostal when I got married in my mid-20s, then returning some years later after a divorce, to my church home that was now non-denominational, having Seventh-Day Adventist siblings, and one daughter who recently Apostolic, there can be several disagreements on interpretations of the Bible. No Denomination is 100% right or wrong. I believe part of the reason God allows the differences is so that we wouldn't walk around like modern Pharisees, full of pride, thinking we know more than Jesus Himself! Besides, our lack of full knowledge will always require us to seek after Him for clarity and understanding till the day we die!

Paul and Peter had a similar religious bout. One minute they were breaking bread together, and the next minute, "Peter and the Gang" were walking out. When Peter's Jewish Christian friends showed up, he began to "feel himself". All of a sudden, he felt it unacceptable to sit at the table with Christian Gentiles because they were not circumcised. His other Jewish Christians agreed and followed behind him. So, Paul, who I'm sure was quite irritated, confronted Peter in front of everybody. He reminded him that the gospel of Christ is not about the law, but grace! It wasn't about the traditions of man, but about the good news of Jesus Christ.

Eventually, Peter came to his Godly senses and went on to spread the gospel, dying a martyr's death upside down on a cross, because he felt unworthy to die the same way as Jesus. Presumably, Paul was killed by decapitation in Rome.

If you are the City of Bethlehem, you are sold out for God. You are sturdy and do not waver. You can agree to disagree and part ways with no loss of love or regret. You're so serious about your walk with Christ that you don't take advantage of time or opportunity to spread the Word of God, through words and actions. You can look over interpretive differences and embrace the commonality of Jesus, his death, burial, resurrection, and seating.

PROPHETIC PRAYER FOR THE CITY OF BETHLEHEM

I do not frustrate the grace of God: for if righteousness come by the law, then Christ is dead in vain. (Galatians 2:21)

Sovereign God, there is no wishy-washy stuff with You. You are solid. It's black or white with You. You don't bend Your way for anybody! You take no lukewarm souls. I have made up my mind to follow You without doubt or any going back and forth. There is no looking back, and I refuse to let others in my space do the same. I will hold them accountable at all costs because I do not worry about how others may feel. When the prideful leave the room to return to the old way, I'll confront them until they come to their biblical senses. It's not that I have things all figured out one hundred percent, but simply because I recognize our commonality in Christ trumps the traditions and assumptions of man. So I will press on to share Your love through Him with the boldness of the power of the Holy Spirit within. In the mighty name of Jesus, I pray, amen.

Chapter 4

CITY OF TEKOA

{Meaning Trumpet, Pitching of Tents}

Fortified by King Rehoboam

Then Abram (Abraham) removed his tent, and came and dwelt in the plain of Mamre, which is Hebron, and built an altar unto the Lord. (Genesis 13:18)

I turned forty in 2007. That year, I received a train trip to the Mall of America in Bloomington, Minnesota as a gift. I went with a group of women who attended the same church. I absolutely loved the train ride. My favorite part was looking out the window at all the different sights along the way. I saw things that before then, I had only witnessed on television, like fishing docks with boats everywhere.

While enjoying my ride, some very unusual things happened. One was meeting a preacher who worked in the kitchen on board. He came to chat with us and shared an autographed prayer book he had written with a few of us. He gave me one because it was my birthday.

The Fortified City

The other out-of-the-ordinary event was an older Caucasian gentleman who got on at a particular stop and began quoting a scripture from the book of Isaiah. To me, he seemed like a very interesting person. He was very odd and unconventional in his appearance, but I felt that his presence was special and added to my birthday getaway. I wanted to know more about him. He was seated in front of me, having a conversation with one of the other ladies in the group, but the seat next to him was empty. I debated in my head for a while as to whether or not I should squeeze by the person sitting next to me to sit next to him. I also wondered what the group would think if I did. I decided to go ahead and sit with him.

I found out his name was Everett and that he lived in the mountains of Minnesota. His teeth were rotted, and his breath was a little tart, but I didn't let that bother me. He was quite surprised that I wanted to sit with him; I could tell by the look on his face. During our chat, I discovered that he was a prophet, and he shared with me that God always works with him using the number forty. I told him it was my fortieth birthday. He smiled and put his head back against the seat, looking as if he was thinking, "You got me again, God." We talked until we arrived in Bloomington. He asked me for my address so he could send me some information we had discussed, and I watched him walk away with a tent on his back. I did hear from him one more time when he sent me the information he promised. I remember him telling me how he would one day die from a gunshot wound to the head in Jerusalem. To this day, I've wondered if he is dead or alive.

Some of us find ourselves hanging out in a tent to be fun. Families camp out with their kids or loved ones at campsites or in their backyards as an inexpensive outdoor adventure. But some people use them for temporary shelter. Homeless people use them to protect themselves from extreme weather conditions and privacy, but others use tents because they allow them to be mobile as well as for typical purposes. Tent revivals are popular during the spring and summer months for outside of the church walls ministry, and Jews celebrate Sukkot (Feast of Tabernacles or Feast of Booths) in the fall with hut-like tents. God spoke to Moses in a tent called the Tabernacle (also known as the Tent of Meeting or Tent of the Congregation). The Bible also metaphorically refers to our body as a tent that houses our soul. But the story of Abram (whose name was later changed to Abraham) speaks of the type of tent to which the city of Tekoa refers.

Abraham moved from place to place, pitching a tent. In Genesis chapter 12, Abraham was commanded to leave his country and relatives and go unto a land that God would show him. The land God promised to show Abram was Canaan (later known as the Promised Land). His obedience to God led to what would be a nomadic lifestyle for him and his wife, Sarai (whose name was changed to Sarah). Some of his tent-pitching sites were Bethel, Hebron, Ai, Mamre, Sodom, and Egypt.

People who represent the city of Tekoa are people who are sent to particular locations for a specific reason, in a specific season. Sometimes they can be viewed as unstable, and if they are in ministry, they can be assumed as "church hoppers. The difference between the church hoppers and the "Tekoanites" is that church hoppers are constantly looking for a physically "perfect" church, which of course, does not exist, although a church can be perfect for the individual seeker.

I can relate to this city as an Evangelist. God has specifically called me as what he told me was a transitional minister. I've never heard this term used by anyone, but I know preachers who fall in this category and may not give it a name. My tent-pitching is usually in seasons of seven or multiples of seven. God uses me to help churches that are transitioning in one aspect or another. They may be establishing a new church or moving to a new location. He uses me as a creative, wherever he sends me to bring about changes to the way things are typically done or seen. Not only does he use me this way in church settings, but also in the workplace and family.

Tent pitchers have to become used to establishing new relationships, being moved in what seems out of season, and being misunderstood. They are usually people who carry a Caleb spirit. In Numbers 14:24, Caleb is described as one having "another spirit with him and he followed me (God) fully, him will I bring into the land whereinto he went; and his seed shall possess it" As the City of Tekoa, you must be confident that God did indeed send you to where you heard Him say go. Although it may be temporary, know that your role while you are there is essential, no matter how small it may seem.

PROPHETIC PRAYER FOR THE CITY OF TEKOA

26) And have made of one blood all nations of men for to dwell on all the face of the earth, and hath determined the times before appointed, and the bounds of their habitation; 27) That they may seek the Lord, if haply they might feel after him, and find him, though he be not far from every one of us: (Acts 17:26-27)

Faithful God, You are my Protector and Redeemer. I cannot begin to count all the many things you have done for me. It would take a lifetime to do such a thing! I count it a joyous occasion to have gone through all the tests and trials of life and come out shining as I do! You clothe Your tent-pitching servants with a creative spirit to do a special work in an assigned location of Your choosing, even when we are comfortable where we currently dwell. I choose to be obedient because I recognize that my choice to follow through has nothing to do with my desires or wishes. I understand that my move is urgent, and staying where I am is not an option. I go without fear! I arrive not knowing my next move, but I rest in You and trust that instruction will come as I continue to read Your Word and pray without ceasing. In Jesus' wonderful name, amen.

Chapter 5

CITY OF GATH

Winepress

Fortified by King Rehoboam

And this your offering shall be reckoned unto you, as though it were the corn of the threshing floor, and as the fulness of the winepress. (Number 18:27)

When I was still a fairly new member of the St. Mark Church of God in Christ, in Wichita, Kansas, there was one Mother of the Church who was good with sharing with the younger ladies of the church, the proper attire both in and outside of the church, as well as many other things women needed to know about presenting ourselves as holy women. Every Thursday, we had night service, similar to Sunday service, minus the choir and formal attire. This particular Thursday was one of those nights that I wanted to be present but not seen. I was a third shifter at the Post Office and was a bit tired from my normal lack of sleep. Mother Jordan was in charge of opening the service. I remember her saying, "I need three people to testify tonight. To testify means to tell of God's goodness in your life. Mother Jordan continued as she began to walk the center aisle, involuntarily volunteering people in the congregation, "You...," she pointed to one and headed my way. I tried at this point to position myself perfectly behind the person in front of me. "You...," she pointed to the second person. Now I just wanted to be invisible as she walked closer to my direction", And you", she said, pointing to me as her third choice to give a testimony. I sighed in my head as I quickly began to think of something to say when it was my turn. The first two people testified right where they stood. But when it was my turn, she stared and pointed at me as if she could see straight through my body and said, "I want you to come up here", as she fingered me in her direction. Of course, I wasn't happy to be called up in front of everybody, but I would never have said so out of respect. I remember mustering up some story of a recent act of God's goodness then sitting back down on the pew and enjoying the rest of the service.

There were several times in my past when I was purposely picked out because I was typically known as a quiet person, and I disliked being tall at times when I wanted to hide. But many years later, long after accepting my call to preach, God took me back to that very day at St. Mark. Mother Jordan had passed away years before God had given me the revelation of my call, but she had been used to usher me right into it. She was a human winepress. Not just her, but many others along the way. Even me at times. Another wine press was my dad. When I was a kid, I was extremely shy, and my father would make me speak to people. I, being a kid, didn't feel it was necessary and hated doing it. Then it was me in Junior High when I tried out for pom-pom and cheerleading, making the squad in my ninth-grade year. Later in High School, I took debate, speech, and forensics all in the same year, to get out of my comfort zone. As God took me down memory lane, I realized that all those "presses" along the way were for a greater purpose.

The Fortified City

If you are The City of Gath, you are a winepress. A winepress is a person or device used to extract juice from crushed grapes by pressing them until nothing is left to smash. The "Gathite" can identify a person who's not exercising to their fullest potential and will push them to do more and be more than they could ever imagine. A coach is a perfect example of a winepress. A mentor, teacher, parent, and body trainer are other examples. You aren't one who easily takes no for an answer, you give really good instructions, and love to see others grow and succeed. Your downfall is taking on the failure of those you help as your fault and responsibility.

God knows exactly who to place in the lives of others to get them to the exact place he desires them to be. He knew he had to equip special people to squeeze the wine, which they possess within them because left to themselves, they would comfortably live under their God-given abilities till the day they die.

PROPHETIC PRAYER FOR THE CITY OF GATH

Iron sharpeneth iron; so a man sharpeneth the countenance of his friend. (Proverbs 27:1)

All-knowing Father God, Creator of both Heaven and Earth. Maker of the Universe. You made me, and You know all there is to know about me. You created me to dominate and excel on this journey called life. My only hindrance is what I allow. You knew many would settle for less than Your original plan was for them, so You kindly made me a winepress to help catapult others into their proper position and placement in this world. I refuse to allow my brothers and sisters to recline on the seat called comfortable. You help me to see the wine bursting to be let out of its confined embodiment. Like a grape, things have been smooth on the outside, but there's juice on the inside! I will crush and smash and press and ignore the complaints of pain. I will not allow them to settle for less than their highest potential, for if I do, I fail on my own. Refresh me to do Your will. Even restore the wine within me that I may press on, one by one, day by day. In Jesus name, the Name above all names, amen.

Chapter 6

CITY OF LACHISH
Invincible or Lion

Fortified by King Rehoboam

The servant (David) slew both the lion and the bear: and this uncircumcised Philistine (Goliath the giant) shall be as one of them, seeing he hath defied the armies of the living God. (1 Sam 17:36)

Who else could fit the bill of courageousness like David? Not many. Although he was nearly overlooked as the one God had chosen to be King, he soon proved himself. There's nothing in the bible that gives David's height, but at the time he defeated Goliath, the almost 10-foot-tall and fierce Philistine giant, he was described as a handsome, red-skinned youth.

Not long before, God had sent the prophet Samuel to Jesse's home, to take a look at his seven sons and point out the one God had chosen to be King Saul's successor. King Saul's disobedience had bruised his rulership, and God had had enough! Samuel arrived at Jesse's home, and each son was presented to him one after the other. By nature, most of us would assume that God would appoint the oldest to kingship, but the bible lets us know in straightforward words that *our ways are not God's way, and our thoughts are not His thoughts* (Isaiah 55:8-9).

After Jesse had brought out the seven sons, it was as if the story would end unsuccessfully. But Samuel asked Jesse one more time if there were any more sons. Jesse admits to having one more son, David, who kept the sheep. This part of the story almost makes me laugh. I say so because most of us know at least one person with a child they'd rather not mention for whatever reason. Oddly, Jesse is mentioned as having only seven sons when David was undoubtedly the eighth. I can't help but wonder if David was considered what we call a mischievous "runt". No matter the reason for him going almost unmentioned, God made clear to Samuel that he does not look at the physical appearance; he looks instead at the heart.

David's young life showed several characteristics that gave him some clear qualifications for kingship. One was that he worked in a field, representing the world and all its problems, or the battleground. Second, he kept sheep, which showed his leadership skills. Thirdly, he fought and killed a lion and a bear long before he killed Goliath, which showed he was not easily shaken and had great confidence. I believe he struggled with a little arrogance as well, but it didn't keep him from loving hard and deeply.

Those who fall under The City of Lachish are fearless! They are frontliners whose slogan is *"Here am I; send me"* (Isaiah 6:8)! You know that there is a thin line between arrogance and Godly confidence, so you work extra hard to stay humble. People who are afraid to stand up for themselves get underneath your skin, and you will sharply make your opinion known when you see injustice. You're comfortable in both the field and the palace!

The Fortified City

PROPHETIC PRAYER FOR THE CITY OF LASCHISH

What shall we then say to these things? If God be for us, who can be against us? (Romans 8:31)

God of all confidence, You possess all power and exude love and mercy. You blanket me under Your protection and keep me safe from all harm. I can depend on you like no other when the rubber meets the road, and I find refuge in your pavilion. I don't have to worry, nor do I have to be afraid, when You are on my side. I can stand against my enemies boldly with Godly courage. I march forward, straight-faced, high steps, and flat-footed until justice prevails. Who cares if no one stands with me wearing earthly clothes? I have a team from heavenly places: The Father, Son, and Holy Ghost! So, I won't back down no matter what the task before me. The weapon may form, but it will not prosper because Jesus shed his blood while enduring the cross. He won, so I win! In Jesus' victorious name, I pray, amen.

Chapter 7

CITY OF AZEKAH
Cultivated Ground

Fortified by King Rehoboam

19) What? know ye not that your body is the temple of the Holy Ghost, which is in you, which ye have of God, and ye are not your own? 20) For ye are bought with a price: therefore glorify God in your body, and your spirit, which are God's. (1 Corinthian 6:19-20)

When I was a child, I watched Jack LaLanne early in the morning before school. I believe he was in his 60's at that time. It amazed me to see a man his age be so limber. LaLanne was on TV from 1951 to 1985. Thirty-four years! He was the first in the nation to open up a public health club, which he did in 1936. He invented the leg extension machine and swam from Alcatraz (an abandoned prison on an island) to Fisherman's Wharf, handcuffed. LaLanne was quite an adventurous busybody for his age. This famous fitness guru died at age 96 due to heart failure from pneumonia. Before that, he had no known illness.

There is a great deal of discipline that goes into staying fit. It's not just about exercise, it's about being consistent, focused, and organized. You also have to watch what foods you eat. We all know the saying "You are what you eat". The bottom line is that we really are what we eat, mentally, physically, emotionally, and spiritually. It requires growth and regrowth through constant pruning and self-cultivation. Cultivating means to prepare for constant development or improve something. So, when we relate that to our bodies, we can understand why taking care of our temple is so important. Above all, as the house of the Holy Spirit!

I admit that this is an area in my life that I struggle to conquer. It's not that God can't help me, but I lack when it comes to my willingness to obey. Ice cream is my biggest weakness. Not only do I love it, but I also eat it slowly to enjoy every bit. I eat fully knowing that it's not good for me, especially right before going to bed. But a disciplined person possessed the ability to turn away from such indulgence. They've learned to prune themselves of unnecessary things. It comes down to mind over matter in situations like this. But how does one get their mind so disciplined? We can do so by exercising our minds. How do we exercise our minds? My answer, of course, is the obvious one: pray without ceasing and read your Bible, including quoting scriptures. Above that, you must be determined to do both.

The wonderful thing about God is that he can help us in every area of our life, including staying focused. He wired us so He knows exactly what will work for each of us. For instance, I'm a number person. I'm always counting even when I don't mean to count. I work very well with a calendar. It's something about writing my goals for the day, week, or month on a calendar where I can see, that helps me. Things will come up, they always do. So I pray and ask God how to adjust and keep moving. Do I stay on task all the time? My answer is no! I wish I could tell you I do, but there are times I get overwhelmed with life, and before I know it, I've gone days or weeks without doing what I'm supposed to do.

God is faithful, and we will always need him, -- no ifs, ands, or buts about it. Our prayers show God that we desire change and are ready to be cultivated by investing in the body of oneself through discipline. "Azekahites" are people who help others become and stay disciplined to maintain or improve their health and well-being. They could be a trainer, a therapist, a holistic practitioner, a nurse, a doctor, or anything along these lines. There are even certain religions and denominations that exercise good eating habits. We must discipline our eating habits to strengthen our bodies and give us the energy to fight physical battles as well as spiritual warfare.

PROPHETIC PRAYER FOR THE CITY OF AZEKAH

That every one of you should know how to possess his vessel in sanctification and honor; (1 Thessalonians 4:4)

Father God, I've come before Your presence with a humble and contrite spirit understanding that You are well able to do what exceeds abundantly above all that I can ask or ever think. My ability to move about is only because You made me capable. I can't even think straight except that You allow me to do so! I have made the decision to take better care of the vessel that clothes my being because I need to be in tip-top shape to run this race called life. I digest the Word to build my spiritual muscle, and I pray to give me strength. But I also eat good physical food to nourish my bones and give myself the energy to do Your will for my life. For if I am granted a long, good life, I must understand that not only is my body the House of the Holy Spirit, but I should not expect Him to make Himself at home in a rickety house that is not up to par. I will be disciplined to a healthy lifestyle by making better choices of the things I eat and the things I drink. Father God, I recognize I can't do this without Your help, but I am both willing and determined. I waved the white flag as I surrendered to You in Jesus' powerful name and I pray, amen.

Chapter 8

CITY OF ARAD
A Wild Ass

Fortified by King Solomon

Being then made free from sin, ye became servants of righteousness. (Romans 6:18)

Paul is one of my favorite people in the Bible. If he had been the lead singer of a singing group, I would have been one of his background singers, repeating every line he sang. I absolutely love the way God used Paul. But knowing his past brings a special light to Paul. He was born in Tarsus around AD 5. Tarsus is in Cilicia, which is modern-day Turkey. He was a Jew with Roman citizenship. Having Roman citizenship gave Paul rights and privileges most people of that day didn't have, like being protected from certain punishments, such as flogging. He also had the right to a fair trial, and if he felt he wasn't treated fairly, he could appeal his case to the emperor. Because of this special citizenship, he could freely and safely travel around the Roman Empire without the same worry that noncitizens faced. When Paul's family moved to Jerusalem, under the teachings of Rabbi

Gamaliel, he learned the Hebrew scriptures and the law of Moses.

After his witness and approval of Stephen's (A Jewish Christian and deacon who was accused of blasphemy for claiming to see Jesus at the right hand of God in Heaven) death by Stoning, Paul began a long run of persecuting Christians. Like a scene out of a Western, Paul mercilessly ambushed Christians in their homes, arresting and imprisoning them. He was all over the place and as wild an untamed horse until God knocked him off his horse (literally). His life changed forever from that moment on.

Paul (who was also known as Saul) was headed to Damascus when he was not only knocked off his horse but blinded for three days by the glorious light of Jesus, who asked him why he chose to persecute Him (meaning Him and the Christians who followed Him). God sent a disciple named Ananias to restore Paul's sight. After this transforming encounter, Paul was sold out for the sake of Christ, going to the highways and hedges and from Jerusalem to Rome, preaching as an evangelist to the Gentiles. His saving hope was that his fellow sisters and brothers would convert to Christianity in the process!

Paul not only preached, but he also exhibited the spiritual gifts of apostolic leadership: evangelism, speaking in tongues (an unknown language spoken to and understood by God), and miracles. He went from being wild about killing Christians to being wild about Jesus and from fleeing Jerusalem to freedom and salvation through Jesus Christ!

My second contestant has no name. He is called The Prodigal Son in the Bible. The Prodigal Son is a fictional person in a parable given to the disciples by Jesus. Parables are short stories that teach moral lessons (AI overview). Two sons were to receive an inheritance from their father. The Prodigal son wanted his share right away. The father agreed and gave him his portion.

The Fortified City

The Prodigal son, with good intentions, left home to experience his dream. He wanted the fast life: women, gambling, partying, and who knows what else. He was having the time of his life until the money ran out. What he thought was freedom, he soon found out was slavery. He knew what he had to do, and he did so reluctantly. Empty-handed and tired, he headed back home, not knowing how he would be received.

Although the brother would soon show himself resentful and underwhelmed, his father spotted him from a distance, ran, fell on his son's neck, and kissed him. Then he clothed him in the finest robe the servants could find, put a ring on his hand, shoes on his feet, and called for a big celebration.

If you are The City of Arad, you are one whose total devotion is to ministry. When you made up your mind to serve God, you never once looked back. You are very transparent when it comes to telling others about your wild past and great turn-around. You tell everybody you encounter in a day's time, about Jesus with no reluctance. Soul-winning is your greatest occupation.

Robin Roundtree

PROPHETIC PRAYER FOR THE CITY OF ARAD

It was meet that we should make merry, and be glad: for this thy brother was dead, and is alive again; and was lost, and is found. (Luke 15:32)

Sweet and Gracious God, You are my eternal love. I don't have to search far to find out that there is nobody on earth like You. You make love so easy and express it so wonderfully by giving Your only precious Son Jesus to die for my sins. I remember the days when I was wild, running the streets like there was no tomorrow, and just living it up and spending money like I had more at home in jars with the lids sealed tight. But the experiences taught me that there is no joy in the things that lead to my demise and the fun is short-lived. Now I know better and will stop wasting time. My life is not my own, and there are places I must go to and things I must do. I have a purpose, and You have a plan for me. I give up and give over my wildlife for You to dispose of. I have grown tired and have aged at sight, but I am ready for a new start. I receive Your mercy and am thankful for Your grace as I put my boxing gloves on and join the fight. I meet my brothers and sisters on the battlefield, fully clothed, to take on the giants of life without fear! The energy I had for the world is now the vigor I have for Christ. I am strengthened as I leave the world behind to flee to freedom through Christ the Lord. In Jesus' name, I pray, amen.

Chapter 9

THE CITY OF HAZOR
Village

Fortified by King Solomon

32) And David said to Abigail, Blessed be the Lord God of Israel, which sent thee this day to meet me: 33) And blessed be thy advice, and blessed be thou, which hast kept me this day from coming to shed blood, and from avenging myself with mine own hand. (1 Samuel 25:32-33)

When I think of a village, two thoughts come to my mind. One of those thoughts is that of the good people in my life who took a hand in helping me become the person I am today. The mothers, including my own, shared wisdom from their life experiences and the Word of God (Bible), as well as friends and family who gave me monetary gifts, groceries, or clothes for my children during the tough times. The women who poured into me with inspiring words when I was struggling to believe in myself.

Secondly, I think about the tribal documentaries I enjoy

watching on YouTube. Most of the time, it is the men of the tribe who go out and hunt for food, and the women who prepare the food. Usually, there is one large pot for cooking all the meats and vegetables. The entire village gathers to eat from the same pot when the food is done. Sometimes the women and men eat separately, chit-chatting amongst themselves, and building relationships. In some of the tribal groups, both adults and children get together for games and singing.

But there are people who are a village all by themselves. Most of us know at least one. All the children of the neighborhood know them. Their house is the one where everyone sits on the porch and hangs out until dark. When I became a mother at age 17, my oldest daughter had a grandmother who lived in an area of our city nicknamed The Boondocks (aka The Boonies). Her name was Mrs. Dee. She had 13 children; most of whom were grown by the time I had met her. She was one of those women who kept her money in her bra. She was very laid back in character but was also lovingly stern and straightforward, the kind that didn't hold her breath about anything.

Everybody in that area knew her, and some of my older siblings had grown up with her oldest children. If I needed help with clothes or school pictures and so forth, she would save up until she had enough and call me on the phone to come pick up whatever it was. She couldn't drive, but somehow always knew everybody's business. She was what we called a heavy-set woman with not one wrinkle on her face. She would sit with her arms folded on her stomach and had a short but hearty laugh. I was told that she once sewed all the cheerleading outfits for a neighborhood youth football team in the area. It was the very same football team that a famous NFL football player played on as a child. I loved Ms. Dee. She was my friend till the end.

I always listen to her advice. I figured someone who

had endured raising all those children by herself knew what he was talking about. She wasn't anywhere close to rich money-wise but had a rich heart. She couldn't work because of some health issues. In fact, she received her college degree in the hospital. I always wanted to do something special for her once I got older and financially able, but the Lord took her home in 2016. My oldest daughter Keiara is so much like her, it's uncanny.

If you are the city of Hazor, you can be a village all by your lonesome! You are a giver. You don't have to ask if there is a need; you see a need and respond. You are the network system within your community, a group, a church, or an organization. You don't have to have much to make things happen, and you don't need any special recognition. Your efforts may get overlooked, but you're not easily replaced. In the workplace or organization, the City of Hazor is the type of person who knows their job front to back and has trained themselves to learn all functions and positions connected to their job. You find work to do without being asked. You easily fill in a spot when there is a "no show" and would rather be home than at work doing nothing. You're like the job Gopher (go for it). Sometimes you can be taken for granted. You do so much that you're often despised because you do so much. You know who you are in Christ and aren't easily offended. You can train new hires and clean the toilets without thinking it's beneath you to do such a thing. You know your worth!

PROPHETIC PRAYER FOR THE CITY OF HAZOR

12) I know both how to be abased, and I know how to abound: every where and in all things I am instructed both to be full and to be hungry, both to abound and to suffer need. 13) I can do all things through Christ which strengthened me. (Philippians 4:12-13)

Most gracious Father God, who can separate us from Your love? The answer is simple: no one! I can search the world and not find a soul that can even begin to be compared to You. It would be a waste of precious time! I long to drink from Your book of strength, and ache to be given just a portion of Your grace. When there is work to be done, I volunteer to fill the shoes that have been left unused because they are tattered and torn. I don't mind as long as they fit. I've worn many shoes and graced my head with many hats, yet I've continued to remain the person You created me to be. I aim to please You in every aspect of service for others without dignified titles for public honor. I know my reward reigns in heaven among the stash of crowns and crisp white robes that await my finish. And I shall not just finish but complete this earthly task with brawn and victory! In Jesus' name, I pray amen.

The Fortified City

The Cities of Refuge

Chapter 10

THE CITY OF REFUGE - KADESH
Holy or Sacred

Fortified by the tribe of Naphtali

20) But ye have not so learned Christ; 21) If so be that you have heard him, and have been taught by him, as the truth is in Jesus: 22)That ye put off concerning the former conversation the old man, which is corrupt according to the deceitful lusts; 23) And be renewed in the spirit of your mind; 24) And that ye put on the new man, which after God is created in righteousness and true holiness.   (Ephesians 4:20-24)

We live in a day and time where purity and holiness have long become bad words. Being a virgin is looked at as primitive, and holiness is considered out of style and unattainable.

In chapter 5, I mentioned the Church Mothers. Church Mothers were very common in predominantly Black churches when I was growing up. Although not as prevalent these days, they are still esteemed as holy, sanctified women who were seasoned with wisdom and stood for righteousness. They would teach you how to sit, bend, and dress, among many other things. They were usually very stern but loving women. If you didn't know any better, you'd be pretty convinced that they had lived their whole lives without sin. They would rarely tell you that they knew when you were fibbing or embellishing about your life. Instead, they would share stories about their past, triumphs, and mistakes, hoping that you would take their advice to heart and follow the path God intended for you to follow. When I think about purity, I think about holiness. Purity is just one aspect of holiness. It's defined as "the state of being set apart from sin and living in a way that reflects God's glory" (AI overview). Holiness is fully surrendering to the will of God. God's will is righteousness. The difference between righteousness and holiness is that righteousness is simply doing what is morally right according to the Word of God, and holiness, in my own words, is divine excellence.

You can be righteous but not divinely excellent. Most of us can think of at least one person who has good morals, even some nonbelievers are morally good. They are law-abiding citizens. They give to charities. They are volunteers for local organizations. They don't drink alcohol, they don't curse, and so on. Overall, they are known as good people. But even with all those good characteristics, they lack the reflection of God's excellence by way of the Holy Spirit, through Jesus Christ. Holiness possesses a maturity that cannot be obtained by just being good. It's an inner and constant yearning to be like Jesus. It's carrying His attributes by your words and actions. Righteousness aims to be holy! Holiness keeps the divine mirror of God ever before you.

If you are The City of Kadesh, your slogan for life is "holiness or hell"! You desire to please God no matter the cost. It comes and remains first, no matter the circumstance. You walk this life alone because there are very few people who want to go above the place of righteousness onward to holiness. You provide a refuge of consistent Godly discipline. You exemplify holiness without judgment towards others because holiness naturally convicts. You help usher others into the deeper depths of God. You know that there are always more and endless levels and revelations of God and possess an inquisitiveness to seek after them wholeheartedly. It's hard for you to understand why Believers lack the desire to go higher, and you're concerned about teaching others the urgency of holiness. As one of the Cities of Refuge, your area of empowerment is what I call disciplined graduation. You help people graduate beyond righteousness to holiness!

PROPHETIC PRAYER FOR THE CITY OF REFUGE-KADESH

Because it is written, Be ye holy; for I am holy. (1 Peter 1:16)

Holy and perfect Father God whose address is Heaven and whose ownership is the universe. Who can begin to understand or figure You out? The answer without a doubt is, no one! You created me with a plan to live a life that reflects Your glorious holiness. With deep sincerity, I desire to walk in its glow in such a way that all the world will be drawn with urgency to know Jesus our Savior and Lord. I walk with my head held high and with no regrets because I willingly choose to dedicate my life to this higher plain of righteousness. As it is written in Psalm 1, I will not walk in the counsel of the ungodly, nor will I stand in the way of the sinners, nor sit in the seat of the scornful. For my delight is in the law of the Lord and I meditate on it both day and night! Because I choose holiness, I shall be like a tree planted by the river that brings forth much fruit and has leaves that won't wither. Thank You that I shall be called blessed as I also prosper, in the excellent name of Jesus' I pray, amen.

Chapter 11

THE CITY OF REFUGE - SHECHEM
Shoulder

Fortified by Jeroboam

26) And as they led him away, they laid upon one Simon, a Cyrenian, coming out of the country, and on him they laid the cross, that he might bear it after Jesus. 27) And there followed him a great company of people, and of women, which also bewailed and lamented him. (Luke 23:26-27)

Minding his own business, just walking along the way towards Calvary, Simon of Cyrene was yanked from a crowd of people to help lessen the weight of the cross for Jesus, who was on his way to endure a gruesome, torturous, agonizing death, being nailed to it. Although there is no physical description of Simon, I can't help but think that there was something about his physique that made the Roman soldiers pick him from the mass of gathered participants. It is said that he walked with Jesus carrying the cross from Antonia Fortress to Calvary, which is about three-fourths of a mile.

The Bible tells us that we should, "bear ye one another's

burdens, and so fulfil the law of Christ" (Galatians 6:2). That means that we should "actively share and help alleviate the difficulties or hardships that others are facing, essentially showing compassion and support to one another in times of need" (AI Overview Google). A burden-bearer must have a willing and humble heart. Our heart symbolizes a compassionate, gentle, nurturing spirit. When we follow our heart, we follow love, and God is love!

Willingness is surrendering our will to selflessness. It's putting our trust in the unseen, realizing we don't have a clue where it will take us once we say yes! The yes is for the good or for not so not-so-good. Either way, it's an adventure. Back in 2011, I retired from the post office on disability due to a work injury and being diagnosed with fibromyalgia, a chronic pain illness. I was happy to get the opportunity to do some things in church that I had been longing to do. One of those things was joining the Congregational Care Department. It was a ministry in the church that visited the sick and shut-in members, whether in their homes, nursing home facilities, or hospitals. One of the congregational care visitors was Mother Neen. I had mentioned to her that I was interested in helping her do the visits. At the time, she had been looking for someone to ride along with her to do weekly visits to thirty-plus members who were unable to attend church either temporarily or permanently, depending on their circumstances. I had no idea that once I gave my yes, within four days I would begin this new endeavor. I admit I was a little afraid at first, and it took some time to "earn my stripes" with this extension of our church family, but my willingness to continue caused me to grow in a different way.

When I mentioned earning my stripes, it was because, during those visits, I learned that you have to be diligent. Older people, in particular, want to know that you are not just some fly-bynighter who wants to boast about something they really don't have the heart for just to make themselves look good or obtain some type of special recognition. My willingness took me to nursing homes that didn't always smell the best. It took me to homes where the furniture didn't match, where I had to avoid sitting or stepping on dog poop. It taught me about Alzheimer's, fatal falls, and how families can divide over who gets what after a loved one passes. I learned to be a CNA without attending one class (not to take the hard work they do lightly). But the flip side was that I established many wonderful relationships and had great experiences. Apart from that, I learned what true evangelism is really about. The Bible says in Romans 10:15, "And how shall they preach, except they be sent? as it is written, how beautiful are the feet of them that preach the gospel of peace, and bring glad tidings of good things!" When you walk into the house or room of someone desiring a shoulder to lean and depend on and lighten their burden with your presence and care, you show the good news of Jesus!

Later, I will talk about being an arm and all the things the arms can do. But what are arms without shoulders? Shoulders support the arms and aid in our ability to rotate our arms in different directions. Shoulders help stabilize the upper part of our body and set our posture. The shoulder symbolically means the ability to bear burdens and carry weight representing responsibility and leadership. So when we bear the burdens of others, we show leadership by stepping in to be the conduit to resources they might not otherwise have, and we show responsibility by being consistent, reliable, and available until the needs are resolved.

If you are The City of Shechem, you possess an extraordinary strength that allows you to take on the burdens of others even when you're going through your own trauma. You would rather be bogged down with someone else's stress than to see them overwhelmed. You are willing to go places others dare not go and do things for people that others don't have the stomach to carry out. "For unto us a child is born, unto us a son is given: and the government shall be upon his shoulder: and his name shall be called Wonderful, Counsellor, The mighty God, the everlasting Father, The Prince of Peace (Isaiah 9:6). Jesus is the ultimate burden-bearer! His shoulders are the only shoulders that withstand the weight of the world and its religious legalism, with His power, His dominion, and His rulership!

Matthew 11:28-30 says, "*28) Come unto me, all ye that labour and are heavy laden, and I will give you rest. 29)Take my yoke upon you and learn of me; for I am meek and lowly in heart: and ye shall find the rest unto your souls. 30) For my yoke is easy, and my burden is light.*" We can find rest knowing that we don't have to do this life alone! His yoke (burden) is easy. All we have to do is submit ourselves to His authority, learn from Him how to rest, and just trust that He has everything under His control.

PROPHETIC PRAYER FOR THE CITY OF REFUGE - SHECHEM

And I will come down and talk with thee there: and I will take of the spirit which is upon thee and put it upon them; and they shall bear the burden of the people with thee, that thou bear it not thyself alone (Numbers 11: 17).

Almighty and Everlasting God, You are the Alpha and You are the Omega. You are the Author of Truth and have existed from infinity to forever. Where can I find such great love other than the one who defines love. My heart is full of feelings I can't explain. I stand as a burden-bearer for my brothers and sisters who cannot carry weight on their own. I rise and volunteer to be the bearer of their burden. I can take it because You built me to share their load by Your Spirit. You taught me exactly how to carry it through Your son Jesus Christ. I walked with Him and learned His ways. I know that as I bear my neighbor's burdens, You will in turn lift my load. I thank You for being so kind and gracious as I ask for Your perfect strength to continue my assignment as a burden-bearing vessel, and I will only go forth in the name of Jesus, my Savior and my Lord. Amen.

Chapter 12

THE CITY OF REFUGE - GOLAN
from gôwlâh meaning captive

Fortified by no one specifically

Thus saith the Lord, the God of Israel; Like these good figs, so will I acknowledge them that are carried away captive of Judah, whom I have sent out of this place into the land of the Chaldeans for their good. (Jeremiah 24:5)

I have heard many ex-convicts say that jail was the best thing that ever happened to them. It wasn't because they enjoyed the time being locked away from the outside world, nor because the food was delectable. It was because it saved their life from destruction. It allowed them the opportunity under very strict confinement, to not only take a good look at themselves, but also for the first time in a long time, hear and see God! These convicts were raised right. They came from good "church families". They knew right from wrong. They served on the usher board or sang in the choir as children. But somewhere along the way, they got off track.

If you are The City of Golan, you give refuge temporarily attributable to captivity. It sounds like an oxymoron to say such a thing, but a place of refuge is not always comfortable or safe. It's more like a bridge because it is somewhat of a passageway from a bad place to a good place. It can even be like a shelter that provides short-term covering. On that narrow bridge or under the temporary shelter, you provide a network of people who are there to support and encourage the captive along the way until they get to a consistently stable place of maturity. During their confinement, if they are paying attention to the bigger picture, they will begin to discover and discern some things about themselves, both good and bad.

To be in captivity according to Collins Dictionary online, means "the state of being imprisoned or enclosed." Other words we may use include confinement, slavery, custody, bondage, duress, and servitude. The Strong's Exhaustive Concordance of the Bible (Copyright 1890 by James Strong) uses the word "Prisoner (from exile) or figuratively a former state of prosperity".

Captivity can affect a person in the following way:

- Mentally - Physically free but can't progress or move forward.
- Physically - Unbearable and agonizing pain. Negatively sensitive to touch.
- Emotionally - Numb, unable to cry, feeling lost, unfit, hopeless, unstable.
- Financially - Struggle to make ends meet, desperate for solutions, and vulnerable to scams.
- Spiritually - doesn't know or understand what God is saying which leads to self-condemnation, regret, and remorse.

The story of Job fits every category of these categories when I think of captivity. Although he was not in a physical jail, he was very much in bondage.

Job was a very just (perfect and upright) man according to the Bible (Job 1:1). He *"feared God, and eschewed (shunned) evil."* God allowed him to be tested by the Devil who was certain Job would curse God during the process. In the course of the test, Job loses all his children, servants, and livestock. All have died due to natural disasters and invasions, all in one day! He humbles himself in great grief over his loss and experiences the torment of Satan physically through painful boils all over his body. To add to his distress, he endured condemnation from three friends, Eliphaz, Zophar, and Bildad who after joining him in a moment in silence, begin to blame him for being sinful as to why he is going through such an excruciating circumstance. He could have been easily scammed into believing all that his "his friends" accused him of if God had not intervened.

"And the Lord turned the captivity of Job when he prayed for his friends: also the Lord gave Job twice as much as he had before" (Job 42:10). God reprimanded the three friends in the end and made them present an offering of seven bullocks and seven rams to Job and offer up a burnt offering which could not be accepted by God until Job prayed for them. This was a sure example of God's mercy upon them, as he would have dealt with them harshly otherwise for speaking of Him as they did (as if they were The God of judgment).

There are many examples of confinement in our communities wherever we live in this great world. I think of hospitals, rehabilitation facilities, nursing homes, crisis centers, and homeless shelters. We can be confined to our homes due to sickness or pregnancy. Captivity is not always the fault of the victim but can still be a time of learning and self-reflection.

Sometimes when we get off track, it's not always, because we have done wrong, it's because we have been wronged by others. Those who find refuge in the person(s) who represents The City of Golan must understand that their arrest and confinement are temporary! As The City of Golan, you aren't the type who is easily swayed or manipulated by sob stories or bribes. You recognize that you have been chosen to help the "inmate" focus and find a Godly solution to their problems so that they won't be as "*dogs returning to their vomit*" (Proverbs 26:11) repeating their mistakes over and over again. On a softer side, you assure them that God hears their pleas for help and that He has sent them to Golan to rescue them from themselves.

Robin Roundtree

PROPHETIC PRAYER FOR THE CITY OF REFUGE - GOLAN

So shall they fear the name of the Lord from the west, and his glory from the rising of the sun. When the enemy shall come in like a flood, the Spirit of the Lord shall lift a standard against him (the enemy). (Isaiah 59:19)

Masterful Father You have never left Your throne. I glorify You as my Abba Father (daddy), realizing that I am incapable of doing anything without You. As The City of Golan, I will help others be set free as You grant me Your strength and mercy. I will teach them how to walk upright and be fearless of men according to Your Word. For what can the Devil do to me unless he is allowed? What can the devil do to them unless You give him permission? I allow You to use me to help others find freedom in captivity. Even in their mess ups I will help them draw back and remember their former days of learning and persuade them to repent. Jesus is our Great Redeemer! The high price has already been paid long ago. So, I will help them to not worry about evildoers, for I know that the standard against the Adversary has been raised so they can walk out free, with double for their trouble in Jesus' Saving name, amen.

Chapter 13

CITY OF REFUGE- HEBRON
Community

Fortified by King Rehoboam

And it was so, that all that saw it said, There was no such deed done nor seen from the day the children of Israel came up out of the land of Egypt unto this day: consider of it, take advice, and speak your minds. (Judges 19:30)

We live in a day and time where tragedy is commonplace. We no longer have to turn on the television to find cold-blooded, unjust killings. They are now in our neighborhoods, shopping centers, and even our churches. Even still, every once in a while, you will hear a story or news report of a death so gruesome or surreal that it brews up a spirit of unrest and anger to a point where people can no longer keep silent or still. Such is the story of the concubine in this text.

    The chapter begins by informing us that there was no king. In fact, Judges 21:25 says that everyone did what *"was right in his own eyes*". This may explain why the Levite man in this text had a concubine and no wife. Now we know that a concubine is like a secondary wife per se. She was of lower status than the wife and was not respected or given the same rights as a wife. In those days, women really depended upon men for survivorship and therefore sometimes would choose to become a concubine as opposed to nothing.

The Bible says that this concubine "*played the whore against*" the Levite (Judges 19:2). Some scholars say that this meant she committed adultery, and others believe she got angry with her husband which may explain why she went home to her father instead of another man. It goes on to say that he went after her to speak friendly to her and bring her home. But things begin to get complicated from that point on.

The father-in-law begs the Levite to stay not once, not twice, but five times before the Levite decides to leave with his concubine. Was it for the daughter's sake to protect her from the Levite or was it for his sake? They left the father-in-law's house heading to the House of the Lord by way of Gibeah when an old man approached them and offered lodging for the whole party! The Levite man accepted the offer and was brought into the old man's home. Sometime shortly after, "men of the city" came to the house and inquired about the Levite man for they wanted to "know" him. To break this down in more understandable language, the men of the city wanted to have "sexual relations" with the Levite. The old man cautioned the men about their lewd desire and offered his daughter and the concubine to compensate. This shows the immorality of the ordeal. On one hand, the old man did not like the wickedness of the city men, but on the other hand, he had no problem turning the woman over to such aggressively vile men. These men took this poor woman, raped and abused her all night and when they were done with her, they let her go. Beaten raped abused and now near death and alone, she returns between dawn and day, to the old man's house and fell at the door grasping onto the doorsill.

You would think when the Levite man opened the door that he would have attempted to rescue his concubine for not only was she someone's daughter, at the least, her Father's daughter! She meant something to somebody. She was someone special to someone. Yet, the Levite man walked past her in all his arrogance and demanded she get up and follow. When she didn't answer (because she was dead) he threw her upon his donkey and took her back to his place where he took a knife and cut her body into twelve pieces and sent one of each piece to the twelve tribes of Israel. The scripture says in verse 30 "No such deed had been done nor seen from the day the children of Israel come up out of the land of Egypt until this day."

In Judges chapter 20 verse 1, *"Israel went out, and the congregation was gathered together as one man."* They first considered the situation. They looked at it from every side. When the Levite was asked for his side of the story, he told them that the men of the city tried to kill him as well as raped and killed his concubine.

After Israel and the congregation gathered all the information, they conferred and took advice from each other and spoke their minds! The voice of the now forever silent victim was heard, just as Abel's blood once cried up from the ground. A war broke out on the concubine's behalf and after several attempts was finally won.

If you are The City of Hebron, you love the community. On any given month, you can be found at town hall events, school board meetings and other special gatherings. You belong to several organizations and have become a household name not necessarily on purpose but because you have been consistent. You fight to have memorials made for those who have been unjustly killed or abused. You stay on the up and up with what's going on in the community and know how to rally in the crowds when needed.

The Fortified City

PROPHETIC PRAYER FOR THE REFUGE CITY-HEBRON

Then spake the Lord to Paul in the night by a vision, Be not afraid, but speak, and hold not thy peace: (Acts 18:9)

God of all, I thank You that the whole world fits in Your hands and I don't have to worry about anything. I have experienced what it's like to put my total trust in You and You have never let me down! When I stand in front of the masses to fight for justice to prevail, I will not be nervous or break a sweat for I know You are with me. Those who have passed on before me will not be forgotten. I will not let it be. I will rally the troops from every direction. I will organize meetings and campaigns and lead them in the streets. I won't give up no matter what. I will fight over and over even if I don't win. As long as silenced voices are heard through me, I consider it a victory! Keep me Lord God and cover me, every day of my life in Jesus' name, amen.

Chapter 14

CITY OF REFUGE-RAMOTH

Heights or High Places

Fortified by King Solomon

And (Esther) said, if it pleased the king, and if I have favour in his sight, and the thing seem right before the king, and I be pleasing in his eyes, let it be written to reverse the letters devised by Haman the son of Hammedatha the Agagite, which is wrote to destroy the Jews which are in all the King's provinces: 6) For how can I endure to see the evil that shall come unto my people? or how can I endure to see the destruction of my kindred? (Esther 8:5-6 KJV)

Funny story. My daughter Keiara and I once had this conversation about a man. She described the man as tall. The things she described to me matched what I said except I described him as being short. Sometime later, I realized that we sure enough were talking about the same man. My daughter is 5'4" and I'm about 5'9". So to me, he was short and to her, he was tall.

Height is all about perspective. At home, where I could see on the top of our refrigerator or on a high shelf, my mom could not. On the other hand, she could easily see the food items in the back of the lowest rack of our refrigerator that I would have to bend myself like a pretzel to see. When we think about height whether we are considered short or tall, we think of something out of our normal reach or something or someone in a high place, based on our point of view. A rich person can be considered in a high place to someone poor. A famous person could be viewed as someone in a high place to someone who is just your everyday Joe or Jill. A few more examples are a CEO or administrator to an employee, a grown-up to a child, and so forth.

In the Bible, Esther was just a typical young lady who was groomed to take the place of Queen Vashti, who had been removed from the position because she had dissipated King Ahasuerus of Persia by not appearing before him to display her beauty to his guests. Esther, unknown to the king, was a Jew. Haman was a court official and advisor to King Ahasuerus. Mordecai was the uncle of Esther who had raised Esther as his own since both her parents were deceased. Hamon absolutely hated Mordecai because he refused to bow down to him. As revenge, Haman sought to kill Mordecai as well as all the Jews in Persia. But Esther, who was now officially queen, stood before the king on behalf of her people, the Jews, to have the letter that ordered the Jews to be killed, reversed! When the king found out the real story behind Hamon's plot, he was hung from the very gallows that he had built, to hang Mordecai.

If you are The City of Ramoth, you stand in the gap on behalf of others. Whether you are a potentate or just someone who is very compassionate about the welfare and livelihood of others, you are a voice of the people and for the people. You will risk your life for the sake of people you know and even those you don't know.

In 2012, there was an assassination attempt on a 13-year-old

Muslim girl by the name of Malala Yousafzai. The Taliban gunmen tried to put an end to Malala's passionate effort to equalize the education in her native Pakistan so that young girls there could have the same opportunities as the young boys did, to attend school. In 2008, the Taliban who were political extremists banned young girls from attending school. Anyone who defied them faced severe consequences. Malala awoke from a 10-day coma and was told by the nurse about the attempt on her life. She had been shot on the left side of her head. She made a critical decision to keep fighting for the right of girls to go to school. Along with her father, she established the Malala Fund to help give girls the opportunity to receive an education. Later, in December 2014, she became the youngest recipient of the Nobel Peace Prize.

Malala is the city of Ramoth. She is an example of a person who has been placed in a high position (high places) and has reached back to make sure others are given a fair chance at life, even at the risk of losing her own life.Those who are the City Ramoth stand on the front line for what they believe, are passionate about the people they fight for, have good, reliable connections (networking system), no fear of man, and are risk-takers.

PROPHETIC PRAYER FOR THE CITY OF REFUGE-RAMOTH

8) Again, the devil taketh him up into an exceeding high mountain, and sheweth him (Jesus) all the kingdoms of the world, and the glory of them; 9) And saith unto him, all these things will I give thee if thou wilt fall down and worship me. 10)Then sayeth Jesus unto him, get thee hence, Satan: for it is written, thou shalt worship the Lord Thy God, and him only shalt thou serve. (Matthew 4: 8-10)

Most gracious Father in Heaven, hallowed it be Thy name. Who can sit me in high places before kings and queens? Who can grant me boldness and clothe me with courage? Who but my Maker? If I stand alone and not with the world, You stand with me! What is the world against me if You are for me? Everything belongs to You and I will never bow down to another god! Did not Your written word encourage my soul and bring life to my bones? Yes! It set me on fire! I can't help the passion within me. I am willing to risk my life even to the point of death on behalf of those who feel they have no voice until justice is done. I will not be moved by threats or acts of violence toward me. I was born to be a martyr so that others can be free. I honorably serve under Your authority, and I worship no one or nothing, living or dead but You. It is in the name above all names, Jesus, that I pray, amen.

Chapter 15

CITY OF REFUGE - BEZER

(Associated with or identified with Bozrah or Boser)

Gold-ore, burning, or torch

Not Fortified

Then I said, I will not make mention of him, nor speak any more in his name. But his word was in mine heart as a burning fire shut up in my bones, and I was weary with forbearing and I could not stay. (Jeremiah 20:9)

Some people are naturally driven. Once they make up their minds to accomplish something, nothing can stop them. But can you imagine being a teenager and having to deliver a message of God to a wayward people? It may not seem like a big deal to most, but we must consider not just his age but his heart. Jeremiah was called the weeping prophet because of his heart towards his people, the Israelites. Yet, despite his insecurities, it was the burning in his heart that ignited the "go" in him. I describe people like Jeremiah as a fireball. A fireball as defined in the Oxford Dictionary, is "a ball of flame or fire, a ball filled with combustibles or explosives, fired at an enemy or an enemy fortification."

The Fortified City

So, if you represent the city of Bezer (Bosor), you are a living walking (portable), explosive, illuminating, intensified, force against the Devil and all his demons (the enemy). You walk in this world like you own it! You set the world on fire! If life's a party you're the reason why! Fire not only dwells in you, but it also forces you to do things the average Holy Ghost-filled Believer would not be confident enough to do.

I remember the first time I did church in the park. The same fire that Jeremiah possessed was in my bones. With permission from my Pastor, I started by sending letters of invitation to several ministers at my church. Unannounced to me, the letters were intercepted by a fellow minister and not sent out. When I found out this happened, the fire in me didn't think twice, I simply called all the speakers, dancers, and so forth, personally, one by one. I asked two musicians if they would be available to help me, but both turned me down for the sake of money. But I knew there were some people who were full of gifts and talents and would share them for free. Don't get me wrong. There is nothing wrong with expecting pay, but there are so many overlooked people who are passionate about Jesus and are just waiting for someone to give them a chance to share their gift and would do it for free. Boy was I right! Every person I called upon from that point on, gladly gave me a yes, but I still didn't know what to do about my need for musicians.

I believe it was my oldest sister Ruby who mentioned that her husband (my brother-in-law Kenny) would probably be willing to loan me two life-size stage speakers. So, I called Kenny up. Not only did he cheerfully loan me the speakers but offered me his keyboard as well. I will never forget and will forever be grateful for his willingness in my time of need. Kenny passed away in November of 2020.

All I needed at that point were microphones, printed signs,

postcards, and bottled water which was covered by my church home at the time, Tabernacle Bible Church Without Walls. We had a wonderful time at McAdams Park that first year. I estimated 50 participants by the end of the week. Not only were my invited participants freely available, but I found out the members of my church who were in the audience came up without question when I asked them to do the prayer and invitation to Christ. One of the church Deaconess, the late Sister Ford, who was more like an Evangelist (to me), would not leave the park grounds until a young lady said yes to Christ. Her quest to get the young lady to accept Christ came long after the event had been dismissed, but I know the Angels in Heaven were joyfully singing at the young lady's acceptance and God was surely smiling upon His Bezer City servant. Sis Ford's passion to see that everyone knows Jesus made her golden!

PROPHETIC PRAYER FOR THE CITY OF REFUGE-BEZER

Father God, You are an All-Consuming Fire. You illuminate the World with Your presence. Anoint us with Your all-consuming fire until I can no longer stand to take any more and I will run and tell the good news all over the world. My heart will express itself out loud. The drive I feel cannot be hindered nor halted. The enemy will come with his agenda and help, but no weapon formed against us shall prosper. I understand the assignment. I am not here to play. My purpose will be accomplished because I possess an unstoppable agenda. Help me to stay humble, because I realize there's a thin line between humility and arrogance. Thank You for the fire. I will carry it like a torch in a dark world. This is my promise, in Jesus' name, amen.

More Fortified Cities to Explore

Chapter 16

CITY OF HESHBON
Stronghold or Fortress

Fortified by the tribe of Reuben

And the lords of the Philistines came up unto her (Delilah), and said unto her, Entice him (Samson), and see wherein his great strength lieth, and by what means we may prevail against him, that we may bind him to afflict him: and we will give thee every one of us eleven hundred pieces of silver. (Judges 16:5)

Spiders, although kind of creepy, are very extraordinary little creatures. They are anthropoids with silk glands, and silk-spinning organs called spinnerets. To build a web, a spider releases silk strings into the air and waits till it attaches to an anchor like a fence or tree branch. From there it doubles down the anchor, making a strong bridge. Midway, it will use its weight to drop down and form triangles one by one, and then it will spin silk around in a circular motion until a web is formed.

Webs are very intricate yet beautiful architecture. It's five times more resilient than steel and two times that of nylon. Spiders will rest on their web and patiently wait for their prey. They don't have the best of sight but can feel the vibrations of their potential victims. The prey is ambushed and injected with digestive juices that cause them to liquify. Next, with such grace and rhythm, they wrap the insect in silk for later consumption. Some spider species will inject after wrapping their victims. Strongholds are like spider webs. In the beginning, they appear to be soft and delicate but can quickly become a living nightmare that without deliverance can completely destroy you.

In the Book of Judges chapter 16, we are introduced to a harlot by the name of Delilah. Delilah, whose name means delicate, was probably the opposite of everything Samson was physically. She was, also most likely, very beautiful, as to why Samson was so smitten with her. The fact that he had intercourse with her proves a spiritual bond as well. Just as spiders can sense the vibrations of their prey before they attack, Delilah consciously detected and took advantage of the vulnerability of Samson who had recently lost his wife to his best friend by way of his father-in-law, who thought Samson to hate her. No doubt Samson was misunderstood, heartbroken, and lonely despite his strength.

Although Samsons' divine power allowed him allowed him to kill a lion with his hands, slew 3,000 military men with the jawbone of a donkey, tie together, and enkindle the tails of foxes resulting in them scattering and destroying the Philistine crops to seek revenge on his father-in-law, nothing would prepare him for the strength of the web in which he would soon find himself entangled. Just as a spider injects his victim with a liquifying substance before the silk wrap, Delilah seduces Samson with manipulation, to tell her the secrets of his strength to the point where he could no longer continue to withhold that his immense strength laid within his long locks of his hair. Three times he had played games between Delilah and the Philistine lords who offered eleven hundred pieces of silver to the harlot to entice Samson. But now he was so worn down, he became numb and unconscious as a liquified spider prey. Soon he found himself a bald and blinded prisoner to these vengeful Philistines who made a sport of him. Standing between two pillars of a house packed with 3,000 men and women, he prayed to God Almighty, one last prayer. The prayer was a plea to be avenged for the loss of his eyes by allowing him divine strength one more time. This gave him the muscle to push the pillars with all his might so the building would cave in and not only kill all its occupants, but himself as well.

"In the Bible, a stronghold is a fortified place of safety or a place where a belief is strongly defended" (AI overview). The Hebraic word for Stronghold is metzuda, which means castle, fortress, or citadel. Just imagine for a moment the massiveness of a castle, the high walls and many rooms. Then imagine being able to hide within it from your enemies. Chances are they wouldn't be able to find you. That's the secure kind of stronghold. Castles are very sturdy and strong buildings, many of which still stand to this day. So, as you can see, there are good strongholds that are used to keep you safe within its walls, and there are bad strongholds that are used to keep you controlled. If you are the City of Heshbon, you provide a safe place from a controlled environment. This could be a Crisis Shelter, a foster parent, a children's home, a friend or family member.

God is our refuge and strength a very present help in trouble. (Psalm 46:1)

The Lord is good, a stronghold in the day of trouble; and he knoweth them that trust him. (Nahum 1:7)

The question is, do you trust that God knows and loves you more than you know and love yourself and can completely deliver us from the tightly gripped claws of Satan? Can you allow Him to be your stronghold and safety? Can you be honest with

Him and admit you have absolutely no control over your situation and cannot deliver nor protect yourself and at times just really don't want to let go other than the fact you know you are not where you should be as far as the path of righteousness goes? If you unball your fist, give up, and look up, the door to your safe place (castle) will open and deliverance will come in the personage of The Everlasting God!

PROPHETIC PRAYER FOR THE CITY OF HESHBON

I will love thee, O Lord, my strength. The Lord is my rock, and my fortress, and my deliverer; my God, my strength, in whom I will trust; my buckler, and the horn of my salvation, and my high tower. (Psalm 18:1-2)

Heavenly Father, there is no one Divine but You! No one is more Powerful or Great as You and no Greater Love than Yours. You define love. How can I even begin to know what love is, lest You teach us? When trouble creeps up on me unaware, or with eyes wide open, only You can deliver me! You are the Cleft Rock I can hide in and the place of safety where I can dwell. No one can totally remove me from my trouble but You. I give up, God! I surrender my all to You! I can do absolutely nothing without You. I've been totally out of control up till now, but I turn myself in and You will strengthen me. I trust You and You lift me out of the miry clay. You shield me from fiery darts. You cover me. You keep me. You save me. I am enabled and encouraged. My future is bright, for You are my light. My going forth is established, for You are my rescuer! Thank you, God, for the victory! I am stuck to you like with strong bonding glue. You did not forget about me. You did not forsake me and for that, I am eternally grateful. In the Redemptive name of Jesus, amen.

Chapter 17

THE CITY OF GEZER

Portion or Isolated area (The Introvert)

Fortified by King Solomon

And the same John had his raiment of camel's hair, and a leathern girdle about his loins; and his meat was locust and wild honey. (Matt 3:4)

When I think about a biblical introvert, I think about John the Baptist. John the Baptist by choice, lived isolated from most of the world, in the Judean wilderness. Reading about him reminds me of the mountain man named Jerome I mentioned earlier. There are things to be said about people who live in secluded areas. Sometimes it is said of them that they are odd and uncivilized. But there are good things to be told of them as well. For one, they can keep a secret well because they don't communicate with outsiders much or hang out in public very often, and when they do, it's with purpose, not to gossip.

Ingram Berg Shavitz, better known as "The Bee Man", is the face of Burt's Bee products. When he was younger, his occupation was a photojournalist. One day, he was taking a picture of an Elderly lady who lived in an apartment and never came outside. Shavitz, out of fear that he would end up the same, packed his belongings and left the big city living of Manhattan to move to the country, in Parkman Maine. He became a beekeeper and began selling gallons of honey on the side of the road. He had a lady friend he had met while living in Manhattan. Her name was Roxanne Quimby. She had moved to Parkman from San Francisco.

Shavitz introduced Quimby to his beehive and honey business and to make a long story short, the business was later incorporated and grew to be worth over one billion dollars today. Burt was bought out for $130,000 by Quimby and went on to live a quiet life even after receiving 4 million dollars from Clorox when they bought the company in 2007. That's just one example of a person who despite having money most would spend on the finer things in life, chose to live off the grid and enjoy a simpler way of life. No, not all introverts and isolated people are rich. Most are trying to make ends meet like most. I just used Burts's story to prove how important it is to live a private and quiet life. Money can't buy that kind of peace.

Those who are The City of Gezer have adopted 1 Thessalonians 4:11 as their slogan, "And that ye study to be quiet, and to do your own business, and to work with your own hands, as we commanded you." They have no problem being alone or having to entertain themselves. They may show up out of the blue to everyone's surprise and don't care to be given any special attention. Birthdays and holidays are just another day for them and gifts, although appreciated, they could do without. "Gezerenes", would rather sit in their yard enjoying pruning their rose bushes or watching squirrels run from tree to tree rather than going for a night in the town with a group of friends. You can air your problems to their ears and not worry about them sharing your secrets with others. They are good listeners, thoughtful, self-motivated, and can be good "out of the box" leaders.

PROPHETIC PRAYER FOR THE CITY OF GEZER

Through desires a man, having separated himself, seeketh and intermeddleth with all wisdom. (Proverbs 18:1)

Father God, You are God all by Yourself and there is no one in all the universe like You. You are the Great I AM, and the evidence of Your presence is all around us. We are never alone. Even when the space around me is full of air and no sign of life, You keep me company. I enjoy my time with You, talk to You all day, and allow You to put me to sleep at night. But I understand that it is not good for a man (or woman) to be alone. So, I make a vow to extend myself to others who may need my ear, my hand, or my heart. I was put in this world not just to open my arms to hug or open my pocket to give a life-changing alm. From this day forward, I will be selfless but remain confident. I will share my space with those who need a good friend and allow some spontaneity and inconveniences to cause me to grow. I will walk the path of Your will only and put away my unwillingness to stretch myself and be more than I ever dreamed I could be. With You guiding me along the way my moves will always be right. Thanks for your help, Lord God. In Jesus name, I pray, amen.

Chapter 18

CITY OF MEGIDDO

Invading, instrument of exposure

Fortified by King Solomon

Then called Esther for Hatach, one of the king's chamberlains, whom he had appointed to attend upon her, and gave him a commandment to Mordecai, to know what it was, and why it was. (Esther 4:5)

I've talked about Queen Esther in a previous chapter, but let's visit her again. Esther had gotten word from her maids and chamberlains that the Jews (her people) were "fasting and weeping and wailing" (Esther 4:3) because of a decree that went out commanding that the Jews be killed. I'm sure Esther's heart fell into her stomach after hearing such a thing, but she needed more information. So, she sent out Hatach, who was one of the chamberlains appointed to her, to do some investigations. He was directed to go speak to her Uncle Mordecai to get all the details. Mordecai had been in mourning, sitting on a street near the king's gate in sackcloth and ashes.

In the Old Testament bible, sackcloth, which was made from black goat hair, was worn in public as a sign of mourning, repentance, and also as an outward expression of humility before God. Ashes were primarily sprinkled on the head or placed as a cross on the forehead or completely covering the body. Mordecai shared with Hatach all about the decree and sent a word back by Hatach to Esther, pleading with her to go before the king.

Here we have two investigators. The original inquirer was Queen Esther, and then by way of her, Hatach. It's like when a news station receives a word that piques interest, to report, and the investigative reporter is sent to research and prepare the report. There are people we know who are good at getting the dish on all the gossip. They don't mind asking the bold questions no one else has the guts to ask. Not only do they investigate, but they expose information that can affect a person or a group of people, whether good or bad.

Hatach may have been the wingman for the investigation but it was Esther who cleverly exposed Haman and his plans. "Megiddoites" are not only somewhat "nosey" but also intrusive. They will go as far as invading what is considered private to some to get a complete story. They are like spies or private detectives. They can take a few rumors, do some deep research, and not only get all the facts but come up with a solution or advice if needed.

Those who fall under the City of Megiddo can be considered annoying and have to be careful not to embellish. On the other hand, like in the case of Esther, it was all for the good of her people that she received the news given by Mordecai because it put in motion the need to save the distressed Jewish people, the Israelites.

PROPHETIC PRAYER FOR THE CITY OF MEGIDDO

13) For such are false apostles, deceitful workers, transforming themselves into the apostles of Christ. 14) And no marvel; for Satan himself is transformed into an angel of light. 15) Therefore, it is no great thing if his ministers also be transformed as the ministers of righteousness; whose end shall be according to their works. (2 Corinthians 11:13-15)

All knowing Father God in heaven, I'm so glad you know me more than I know myself. That gives me a sense of peace because I realize that for any problem I have, You have a resolution, and for all my worries and fears, You are my place of rest. I thank You for every discovery revealed and every mystery uncovered when I come in contact with situations that cause me to have to look a little deeper for the sake and welfare of others. I will choose to mind my own business and tend to my own affairs when what I hear is just a rumor or gossip that appeases itching ears. I find no joy in seeking information and exposing it to the detriment of Godly people and will always treat others as I desire to be treated. In Jesus name, amen.

Chapter 19

THE CITY OF GEBA
The Hill

Fortified by Asa

6) And she said to the king, It was a true report that I heard in mine own land of thy acts and of thy wisdom. 7) Howbeit I believed not the words, until I came, and mine eyes had seen it: and, behold, the half was not told me: thy wisdom and prosperity exceedeth the fame which I heard. (1 Kings 10:6-7)

Beverly Hills, Brentwood, Orinda, Hillsborough, and Atherton, California are just five of several exclusively wealthy residential areas in the United States that are actually located in the hills. Some others outside California are Cherry Hills Village, Colorado, Highland Park, Texas, and Short Hills, New Jersey. There are many reasons why the rich prefer these hilly areas over the flat lands. Among the reasons are the stunning views, privacy, and plenty of space or land, peace and prestige. Hills give the rich the "better than you" stance. If you want to be like them, you must come up!

The Fortified City

King Solomon was the wealthiest man ever to live on earth. His riches would far bypass all the richest men and women on earth. It is said that his net worth today would be 2.1 trillion according to standcourageous.com. But there is no price you could pay for the wisdom he had. Those who study the Bible know that it was because King Solomon asked for wisdom instead of wealth as to why God blessed him to be the richest man in the world as well as the wisest. However, his greatest downfall, in my opinion, was his weakness for women. Having a harem of 700 wives and 300 concubines (what we call a common-law wife in modern-day terms). King Solomon's palace was on Mount Moriah which was a hill. Just for your information, Mount Moriah is set inside the Islamic Dome of the Rock today.

I talked about the City of Ramoth in Chapter 14, but the high place mentioned in that chapter was positional meaning the people at that level weren't necessarily rich. Metaphorically the "hill" is a wealthy status. It's a person who is used to living a certain way and can afford it! They are people who can teach you about business and managing finances. They can connect you to a network of people who can back you up financially and give a hand up instead of just a handout. They can teach you how to become financially sound and independent. The hill takes wisdom to maintain its status. King Solomon possessed the wisdom he needed to maintain both family and riches as well as his duties as king.

Queen of Sheba had heard about this rich and famous King Solomon and traveled to the palace for a visit with him and to test his wisdom. She bought a large entourage with her and gifts of jewels, all kinds of spices, and gold. She asked King Solomon a series of questions and he answered each one of them which greatly impressed her. She was overwhelmed with everything about the King, his wisdom, his palace, the food, and all his workers.

People of the Hill are well-to-do and aim higher, never settling for less. They understand that God "wishes above all things that [they] would prosper and be in good health even as [their] soul prospers (3 John 2 paraphrased)." They will reach down and pull you up but never allow you to pull them down. They are investors who know the money game and are wise with their moves.

Take note that even wisdom has to be used wisely, or you can lose everything you worked so hard to obtain. Although Solomon was very rich and full of wisdom, his self-indulgence proved that he did not always use wisdom wisely. He appeased the desires of his foreign wives by building altars to false gods on surrounding hills (1 Kings 11:1-8). This angered God. After all, God was the one who blessed him with such abundance!

The Fortified City

PROPHETIC PRAYER FOR THE CITY OF GEBA

17) Charge them that are rich in this world, that they be not highminded, or trust in uncertain riches, but in the living God, who giveth us richly all things to enjoy; 18) That they do good, that they be rich in good works, ready to distribute, willing to communicate; 19) Laying up in store for themselves a good foundation against the time to come, that they may lay hold on eternal life. (1 Timothy 6:17-19)

Everlasting Father, You reign from infinity to forever. You own cattle on a thousand hills. The earth is Yours and all that dwells therein. As the City of Geba, I ask for wisdom, and I choose to be careful. You have blessed me to obtain more than I ever dreamed. I may not be the richest, but Your wisdom leads me to make Godly choices in all that I do. I choose not to move unless You direct me to do so. I aim to increase in everything You bless me to do. Money, land, wisdom, knowledge, whatever You give me, I will multiply and give back to You from the top and freshest produce. I promise to reach down and pull others up who have never experienced the lifestyle of the hill. I refuse to be jealous, arrogant or turn my nose up when they become my neighbor. I will not let money or any other thing be or become my God. In Jesus name, amen.

Chapter 20

CITY OF MIZPAH
Watchtower

Fortified by King Asa

The people which sat in darkness saw great light; and to them which sat in the region and shadow of death light is sprung up. (Matthew 4:16)

Lighthouses are very beautiful towers of light. Their history and purpose are quite interesting. The earliest history recorded dates back to 247 B.C. It was called The Lighthouse of Alexandria (also known as the Pharos of Alexandria). It was made of white marble and had three floors. It was designed and built by Sostratus of Cnidus (a Greek architect and engineer) on the Island of Pharos and was commissioned by Ptolemy I Sotor, who was King of Egypt at the time but completed by his son (Ptolemy II). Over the years to come it would be damaged by a series of earthquakes, abandoned, and eventually completely demolished in 1480.

Lighthouses today are somewhat automated but still require management by Lighthouse Keepers. There are three types of lighthouses; land-based, offshore, and lighthouses with specific purposes. Some land-based lighthouses have stations. The stations include living quarters for the keeper, a fuel house, a fog signaling building, and a boat house. The lighthouse that we typically see in magazines, calendars, and pictures, has a lantern room that houses a single rotating light. What appears to us to be a blinking light is actually a Fresnel light. Augustin Jean Fresnel, a civil engineer and physicist from Broglie, France, created a flat lens with stair-step prism effect, that replaced the convex lens which was too heavy and expensive. This effect was revolutionary because it redirected the single light beam and magnified the lights causing it to be seen by Mariners from a further distance. When this light is rotated it gives a blinking movement.

A Sector Lighthouse served a different purpose. It has no lantern room and uses "a specialized lens system to project distinct colored beams of light in different sectors. These color code lights help by navigating ships and other water traffic safely. Lighthouses protect by shining on the waters to not only show which way to go but also where danger lurks. Some people provide the same kind of protection. They are the City of Mizpah; Watchtowers. Watchtowers were created to guard and survey a particular place or area. They protect from enemies with a defense system of some type of communication and weaponry. Historically, they were usually the first line of defense against rivals.

People who fall under this city don't play about the safety of the people they are employed by or love. They will go as far as risking their own lives to save the lives of others. They are fathers, mothers, siblings, bodyguards, emergency responders, and the military. They are fearless at least in the moment they need to be. They have eagle eyes and don't trust others easily.

They are always aware of their surroundings and yours too. Their presence makes you feel safe and secure.

By now you should understand why your light cannot be hidden. Know that you are not anything less than important in this journey called life and understand that your ability to shine comes from the Great Creator and Light of all that shines, the Ever-illuminating, Majestic, Almighty, God! Life with God is obtainable through his Son (Sun), Jesus who is The Christ (The Anointed One) and Savior (One Who protects, rescues, and saves us from all evil) of the world!

PROPHETIC PRAYER FOR THE CITY OF MIZPAH

The LORD is my light and my salvation; whom shall I fear? The LORD is the strength of my life; of whom shall I be afraid? (Psalm 27:1)

Awesome God, I thank You for Your presence and Your patience with me. Where can I go on earth or sky and You not be there? I don't really want to know. Where can I hide and You not find me? Nowhere. Darkness runs from You and the rain dries up. Pathways obey and clear the way so we can see which way to go. I know where to turn, what to avoid, and can see how far I am away from my destination. It may take a while to get there but I will make it because Your light keeps me safe. We are strengthened knowing I don't have to be afraid because as long as I follow Your will You will protect me from my enemies. I will rest in You as I turn the helm Your way. I will sail to shore and take Your hand as I safely alight my ship. Bless me, Lord, to walk in Your light and stay in Your sight. I will be forever honored and grateful! In Jesus' saving name, amen.

Chapter 21

CITY OF NAZARETH
Branch

Not Fortified

In the mountain of the height of Israel will I plant it (a cedar twig): and it shall bring forth boughs, and bear fruit, and be a goodly cedar: and under it shall dwell all fowl of every wing; in the shadow of the branches thereof shall they dwell. (Ezekiel 17:23)

Parasitic birds are birds who lay their eggs in the nest of other birds, to be born, fed, and nurtured. The birds who care for these "foster chicks" are known as host birds.

Parasitic birds not only abandon their babies before birth, except facultative brood parasitic birds, who typically make their nests, the parasitic birds are actually "bully birds". Among them, there are Cuckoos, Indigo, and Whydahs which are in Africa. Not only do they leave their eggs for other birds to raise, but some will purposely destroy the eggs or chicklings of host birds so that their babies are given full-time attention and care. Don't be surprised to see a bird as small as a hummingbird taking care of a parasitic baby three times its size! Parasitic birds have strong muscles in their backs as newborns. Even before they gain their sight, they use their back muscles to push out the eggs or babies of the host (mother) bird right in their sight.

We all know someone who has the characteristics of a host bird. It may be you. If you are the City of Nazareth, you are the type of person who cares for those who are neglected or abandoned. You are willing to take them in and treat them as your own. I remember a story my mother, Eddis Roundtree told me about four children in their neighborhood (when they were raising my older siblings) whose mother ran the street. When I say, "ran the streets", I mean she spent her days in and out of the homes of different men, leaving the children to roam the neighborhood on their own. My mother was one of a few mothers who would take them in, wash them up, and feed them. Early in their marriage, it was normal on any given day for my dad to come home and find extra little ones at the table.

Nazareth means branch. One relatable definition of the word branch is defined as, "a part of a tree that grows out from the trunk or from a bough" (the main branch of a tree) (Oxford Languages online). There are so many biological details about branches and the whole science about trees that it could get us off focus. We will just stick to the spiritual basics as it relates to you as a city. To say it simply, branches are arms. Just as branches extend from the trunk of a tree, so do those of us who possess this city, as arms of God.

Our arms can do so many things. They can help us push, pull, lift, lower, reach, raise, and hug.

PUSH

Through thee we will push down our enemies; through thy name will tread them under that rise up against us. (Psalm 44:5)

As the city of Nazareth, you, through the help of the Lord, protect your people by keeping them safe from their enemies.

I'm not just talking about human enemies, I'm also talking about anything that causes them harm physically, mentally, emotionally, or spiritually. For instance, if your person struggles with alcohol addiction, then you protect them by not bringing liquor around them. If they are becoming too comfortable with not attending church regularly, then you help them by making sure they attend and that excuses are unacceptable unless they are sick or dying. We push the enemy away with our arms both spiritually and literally. Our prayers against the enemy, better known as warfare prayers, are how you help your city habitants to be safe.

PULL

And he took him by the right hand, and lifted him up: and immediately his feet and ankle bones received strength. (Acts 3:7)

This passage does not include the word pull, but there is something very interesting about it. We all know that lifting someone to a standing position with their hands involves a pulling of the arms. But the Greek meaning of the word lift helps the scripture take on quite a different perspective. According to the New Strong's Exhaustive Concordance of the Bible (Nelsons) Egeiro, the Greek word for lifted means "to wake or awaken, also to rouse from sleep, sitting lying, or from disease, from death, or figuratively from obscurity, inactivity, ruins, and non-existence."

The indwellers of your city receive life. They are given a new start because you see them. When they feel non-existent from others, you give them a lift. A leg up! You woke them up from their state of death when all seemed hopeless.

HUG

Now the eyes of Israel were dim age, so that he could not see. And he brought them near unto him; and he kissed them, and embraced them. (Genesis

48:10)

In this verse, there is a very special embrace. It's not just about two sons or two tribes, it's about the meaning behind their names. Manasseh means to forget, and Ephraim means fruitful. Israel has an argumentative meaning among scholars. Included are God's fight, God prevails, and one who wrestles and struggles with God.

As the City of Nazareth, you embrace the downtrodden and you open not only the doors to your heart, it shows (realness)! You cause them to forget the hurt and sorrow they have endured and embrace the fruitfulness of life abundantly. Your hug has the compassion that others are missing. It shows the overflowing love of God and his prevailingness.

LOWER AND LIFT

11) And it came to pass, when Moses held his hands, that Israel prevailed: and when he let down his hand, Amalek prevailed. 12) But Moses hands were heavy; and they took a stone, and put it under him, and he sat thereon; and Aaron and Hur stayed up his hands, the one on the one side, and the other on the other side; and his hands remained steady until the going down of the sun. (Exodus 17:11-12)

You at times will become exhausted in your constant attempts to lift others. As others win their personal victories, though your underlying desire is to never give up on them, you will find that you also need the support of others. Your support system will have to be of similar city attributes. They will have to possess strength, be dependable, and be determined to stick it out (endure) with you. You can trust them because the love of God is in them. They will understand that your desire to see others victorious is not just your duty but your passion! It's a domino effect in the end. We will need a shoulder of someone to lean on to help us be who God created us to be.

THE EVERLASTING ARMS

The eternal God is thy refuge, and underneath are the everlasting arms: and he shall thrust out the enemy before thee; and shall say, Destroy them. (Deuteronomy 33:27)

Who is the Eternal God? In this scripture reference, the Hebrew word for eternal is qedem (keh'dem) which in short means from or the East. Ultimately God is not a god-like Dagon or Melech or some other man-made God who comes from the East where the sun rises from eternity.

Before sin, the East was a symbol of Holiness. The Garden of Eden was located in the East of Eden, and the entrance to it also faced the East. But after sin, after Adam and Eve left the garden, the East, what was originally a place of safety and security, became a place of exile. It became a place of the wilderness from which destructive winds came.

So why, if the East was now a negative thing; a wilderness, and exile, a disconnection from God, why is the Eternal God still the God of the East? I asked God, and before I could finish asking Him, he gave me a knowing. He said, "I am still the God from eternity even in the wilderness and desolate places of your life". You may say, "Well is He not the God of the West?", and I tell you this, God is not only the East God that's there in the sun rising moments of your life, He is also the God who is there when the lights go out and it becomes dark. "Where is he in the dark?' you say. There's a song chorus that says, "I can see Him shining, Through the trees, and the wind, and the breeze. I can see Him shining, Thru the night and the stars that glow so bright...." We can be comforted in knowing he is there wherever "there" is for you, at any given moment. Revelations 1:8 says, "I am the Alpha and Omega, the beginning and the end, saith the

The Fortified City

Lord, which is, and which was, which is to come, the Almighty."
He is the East and the West, the sunrise and sunset!

"The Eternal God is our refuge..." The Hebrew word for refuge is maon (maw-ohn) which means a dwelling place, habitation, or den.

Some of us have or grew up in homes that had a den. It was the one room in the house where everyone could hang out and relax. God is our dwelling place, our den, our refuge.

"The eternal God is our refuge and underneath are the everlasting arms". Where is underneath? Underneath is where we bottom out. It's the place we get to in our lives where we feel like we can't be reached. The desolate place where darkness exists, the wilderness, the place where it seems there's nowhere out unless God finds us! It's the place where you ask, "God, do you see me?" We don't have to wait for God to show up. He is already "there". When we are at our bottom, God's everlasting arms are right underneath!

What's in the everlasting arms? What do we get out of His arms that I can't get out of the physical arms of a man or woman, or boy or girl? The Hebrew word for arms in this text is zrowa (zer-o'-ah) and means mighty power, shoulder, and strength. God's everlasting arms possess might, power, and strength, and can be a shoulder to lean on. It makes me think of the hymn, "Leaning on the Everlasting Arms". (Hoffman & Showalter) One of the verses says, "What have I to dread, what have I to fear, I'm leaning on the everlasting arms." His arms are as shoulders and his strength, power, and might are underneath our lowest point!

We're all a part of God's earthly arms but when we can't find earthly arms, we know that we can dwell, hang out, and relax in God's everlasting arms.

Within Thy Circling power I stand;

On every side I find Thy hand;

Awake, asleep, at home, abroad,

I am surrounded still with God.

Written by Isaac Watts
(from Psalm 139 part 1 - allpoetry.com)

PROPHETIC PRAYER FOR THE CITY OF NAZARETH

Thy people also shall be all righteous: they shall inherit the land for ever, the branch of planting, the work of my hands, that I may be glorified. (Isaiah 60:21)

Heavenly Father, You are so gracious and merciful to us. You cannot be compared to any earthly thing. You can never be defined or confined. You are God all by Yourself. Thank You, Father. Forgive us for all our sins and help keep us on the straight and narrow way, in Jesus' name. Those among us who identify as the City of Nazareth shall "inherit the land for ever" and be a branch; an arm of God's planting; the work of His hands, extending to the ill-treated and outcast, so that they may raise from dead places and be revived and that You may be glorified. In Jesus' name, amen.

Chapter 22

THE INVITATION

I was driving down the highway one day and as I exited on the ramp heading to my destination, I saw a small sign in an empty field with the words "Jesus Loves You" followed by a phone number. I have known God for as long as I can remember and my relationship with Jesus started early in my life. But this sign provoked a thought in my mind. I have never heard that Krishna (Hare Krishna) loved me, I never heard that the gods of Buddhism or Hinduism or any other earthly god loved me. What I have heard all my life is that Jesus loves me, I even sang it in church as a child. I learned from reading the Bible that God is love. He defines it and grants us an extension of it not only through the example of Jesus but through the comfort, conviction, direction, and guidance of the Holy Spirit which is the Holy breath of God that dwells within those who believe that Jesus endured and died on the cross, was buried, arose from the dead and is seated on the right hand (side) of God.

My heart gets excited and bubbles up with joy every time I think about what he has done for me (personally). I desire you to feel that same way. I want you to know that there are many "gods" in the world, but none will love you. The God of the Believer (someone who believes in Jesus the son of God) is the

God of all! He always was, He always is and He always will be. He has no birthdate and there is no death date for Him on a tombstone somewhere. He is God the Father, God the Son (Jesus), and God the Holy Spirit all in one. He shares Himself as a team (or company) of three to show that although He could operate all by Himself, He exercises as a company and desires you to know that you are not meant to be nor are ever alone! You may say, "But I have no friends, I have no family". Know with God you can have three BFF's (Best Friends Forever) and his forever is not till death. It's forever meaning without a number limitation (infinity).

So, what do you need to do to have the Omni-potent (All-Powerful) God in your life? It's really simple. Accept His Son Jesus into your life! God gave Jesus (His ONLY Son) to the world. Jesus is the person (of the three in one) of God who came down to earth and was born through a young virgin named Mary who was engaged to a man named Joseph. Her conception was a divine one. God specifically chose her and placed Jesus within her. In other words, she never had intercourse earthly or divine-wise. She and Joseph were told of this immaculate conception by an Angel.

Jesus was born and lived a sinless life. You may say "How so?" Because He is of God, he cannot sin. He was on earth for thirty-three years teaching and performing miracles of healing and deliverance. But his main reason for coming was to die for our sins (wrongdoings) so that we would not be doomed to hell. He took a long gruesome journey with an extremely weighty cross on his back. Whipped, spat on, and beaten, until he resembled raw meat, he then was nailed (both hand and feet) to the rough, prickly rugged cross He had carried. While wearing a crown made of thorns that had been jabbed down on his head, he took on the sins of the world (sins of every human being). He did all that to give us access to God and to the beautiful place called heaven. He hung there for six long hours. Yes, I said six! They mocked Him. They gave Him vinegar to drink for his thirst with pleasure. But he still prayed to God, "Forgive them for they know not what they do." (Luke 23:34)

What kind of love endures such pain and humiliation? A Christ who loves me. A Christ who loves you! After those long agonizing hours on the Cross, he died. Yes, a real earthly death! But it didn't end there. Three days later, he did as he promised and rose from the grave, spent forty days on earth and then ascended back to His home beyond the clouds, and took his place on his throne next to Father God.

So, there's the short version of a long story. I had to share it with you because I need you to understand and make the absolutely most important decision that you will ever make in your life! It's most important because there are only two places you go when you leave here. One is Heaven and the other is hell. Both are eternal but only one is good. That's Heaven! Denominations will argue about how you get there but let me make it clear, no Denomination is 100% correct. I think God allowed these arguments because if we had all the right answers in this life, we would neglect to seek him and study His Word. God is God and we are not! The Bible says, "For my thoughts are not your thoughts, neither are your ways my ways, saith the LORD. For as the heavens are higher than the earth, so are my ways (Isaiah 55:8-9). At the end of the day, it's not about the "how" we get there, it's about the "that" we get there.

I plead with you to accept Jesus into your life and into your heart. He is the ONLY way to eternal life with God in Heaven. Say this prayer and your life will forever be changed. You will never be the same.

The Fortified City

Dear Father God, Yes You are my Father God, the one who created me. I believe You exist and I believe in Your son Jesus. Jesus, I believe in You. I believe that You lived on earth, died on the Cross for my sins, was buried in a tomb, and rose from the dead three days later. I believe that You ascended to Heaven and are seated next to Father God. You are my door to Father God. I admit I am a sinner and up till now my life has been a mess! I repent (confessing and turning away from) of my sinful life. Please forgive me, Jesus, for all my past sins. I've been looking for love in all the wrong places, but now I know You love me Jesus and you possess a love for me that I will never fully understand but desire to experience. I realize that I don't have to wait till I get better or get everything right before I come to You. I get that I can't get things right without You. You are my Lord and You are my Savior. I give my life to You today and I choose to live for and serve You for the rest of my life! Thank You Jesus, for enduring the Cross for me! I love You. Teach me how to live my new life in You. Amen.

For God so loved the world, that he gave his only begotten Son, that whosoever believeth in him should not perish, but have everlasting life. (John 3:16)

ABOUT THE AUTHOR

Robin B Roundtree is an Evangelist, a Creative Freelancer, and an entrepreneur, born and raised in Wichita, Kansas. In almost 25 years of ministry and as founder of Project: Can Anything Good Come from the Hood (based on the Bible verse John 1:46), she has demonstrated her special call to those who are overlooked, allowing them opportunity to display their gifts and talents through expressive arts like, skits, praise dance and singing. With faith and family as her greatest support, she continues to be both hands and feet in the mission field, helping those in need by going into the highways and hedges where the harvest is plentiful, but where the laborers are few.

www.ingramcontent.com/pod-product-compliance
Lightning Source LLC
Chambersburg PA
CBHW030944090426
42737CB00007B/539